# REAL-LIFE MATH INVESTIGATIONS

by Martin Lee and Marcia Miller

**30 activities
that apply
mathematical
thinking to
real-life
situations**

SCHOLASTIC
**PROFESSIONAL BOOKS**

New York • Toronto • London • Auckland • Sydney

To Saul, who has zillions of real-life math investigations ahead of him.

Cover design by Jaime Lucero and Vincent Ceci
Interior design by Sydney Wright
Cover photos supplied by Super Stock
Photo research by Nia Krikellas

ISBN 0-590-96384-8

**D**ear Teachers,

We know you're always looking for high-octane activities you can use to add new sparks to your math classes. So we asked ourselves what excites us about math and gets our creative juices flowing. For us, it's a puzzling situation to explore or an unexpected question we're curious to answer. Our experience is that the same holds true for students.

We've created these investigations so students can recognize some of the math in the world around them. As they dive in, they'll get to sharpen their reasoning powers, reveal their creativity, apply math ideas, and have fun at the same time.

Happy investigating!

Marcia Miller and Marty Lee

# ☼Contents

## TIME AND MONEY

## SIZE AND SHAPE

# HOW MUCH? HOW MANY? HOW FAR?

# APPENDIX

# About This Book

In its *Curriculum and Evaluation Standards for School Mathematics*, the National Council of Teachers of Mathematics (NCTM) urges teachers to help students become confident independent thinkers and mathematical problem solvers. Math educators value the importance of helping students improve their reasoning skills, develop mathematical insights, and engage in mathematical communication. Good math investigations support these goals by providing students with opportunities to explore, discuss, strategize, reason, predict, discover relationships, interpret, conclude, and reflect. A teaching approach that uses investigations helps students appreciate the usefulness of mathematics in the world.

In the real world, mathematics isn't rows of exercises; nor situations created just to practice isolated concepts or skills. Real-life math can be a mystery to solve, a task to plan, a question to answer, a situation to quantify, or data to analyze. Investigation situations aren't necessarily linked to a certain math concept or skill ("So I multiply to solve this, right?"). Rather, investigations, by their very nature, demand an open-minded, multifaceted approach. In general, they call upon students to set goals, ask questions, gather data, make and verify calculations, and communicate their findings. Investigations require creativity, flexible thinking, and an ability to adjust assumptions or try new methods.

In the real world, mathematicians bring all their skills to an investigation. They don't first decide what operation to use or whether to use a calculator or paper and pencil to compute answers. First they get their minds around the problem. They evaluate what they know and determine what they need to know. They decide how to break the task into reasonable parts, figure out what to do with those parts, and plan how to put them back together again. Finally, they draw conclusions from their findings and present the information to colleagues, clients, or students.

Each investigation in this book asks a question and presents a plan of action. None has a single "right answer," yet all can be answered in some way. There's no answer key—it's up to students to use their critical thinking skills and number sense to evaluate their work and the work of their classmates. It's up to you to help them recognize and apply the math ideas embedded in every investigation, such as patterns and relationships, computation, estimation, measurement, statistics, and proportional reasoning.

The Appendix of the book offers additional ideas for investigations, as well as generic reproducibles you can provide to students as they investigate.

# Teacher Tips

○ Each investigation has a teacher page with guidelines to help you facilitate the task, and a page written directly to students. Note, however, that the student page is not a recipe. Rather, it is a broad structure that encourages creativity and allows students to find their own investigative methods.

○ Adjust any investigation as you see fit. For instance, if an investigation involves public transportation and you teach in an area that does not provide this service, change the goal of the investigation to suit your circumstances.

○ Most investigations lend themselves to collaboration and cooperative learning. However, feel free to determine the best grouping to suit your teaching style and the learning styles of your students. Students can investigate individually, in pairs, in small groups, or even as an entire class.

○ Provide Investigator's Logs and Investigator's Wrap-Ups (pages 80 and 81) for each investigation. Students can use them to take notes, collect ideas, make sketches, record their own questions, and reflect on their learning after they finish. Students can compile the sheets in an Investigator's Portfolio.

○ Use the investigations as classwork, homework, or projects. You can have students select investigations they wish to pursue, or you can assign them. You might also use the investigations as performance assessments.

○ As students share their findings, encourage classmates to acknowledge and respect the variety of solution methods and presentations that emerge. Because strategies can be so diverse, the quality of the outcomes will vary. Encourage critical thinking by guiding students to question incomplete solutions or conclusions that don't fit the facts.

○ Take time to join an investigation team yourself. Students can benefit from seeing you in the role of investigator. They'll realize that there are things you don't know but attempt to figure out by planning and following a course of action. Ask questions and give hints. Your active participation can help students to become more confident, successful independent thinkers.

○ Involve parents! Present investigations at parent meetings to demonstrate one more approach that's part of your math program. Some investigations may be ideal activities for workshops, to help parents understand the process involved in this kind of investigative thinking.

# NCTM Standards

| | LESSONS | Number and Number Relationships | Number Systems and Number Theory | Computation and Estimation |
|---|---|:---:|:---:|:---:|
| **Time and Money** | A Year is . . . | ● | ● | ● |
| | Buying Sneakers | | ● | ● |
| | Cash Comparison | ● | ● | |
| | Line of Fries | ● | ● | ● |
| | Party Sampler | ● | ● | ● |
| | Home for Sale | ● | ● | ● |
| | Classified Information | ● | ● | ● |
| | On-Air Analysis | ● | ● | ● |
| | Inflation Summation | ● | ● | ● |
| | Creating an Impression | ● | ● | |
| **Size and Shape** | Eggs-amination | | ● | ● |
| | Package Deal | | | ● |
| | Composite Car | | | |
| | Tile In Style | ● | | ● |
| | Play Space | ● | | ● |
| | Tower Power | | | ● |
| | On a Roll | ● | ● | ● |
| | Best Foot Forward | ● | ● | ● |
| | Left Or Right? | ● | ● | ● |
| | The Ideal Athlete | ● | ● | ● |
| **How Much? How Many? How Far?** | Dairy Diary | ● | ● | ● |
| | Under Cover | ● | ● | ● |
| | Go with The Flow | ● | ● | ● |
| | What's Inside? | ● | ● | ● |
| | Counting The Uncountable | ● | | ● |
| | Bus Stop | ● | ● | ● |
| | On The Road | ● | ● | ● |
| | Stating Data | ● | ● | ● |
| | Run And Jump | ● | ● | ● |
| | Fold And Fly | ● | ● | ● |

● Every investigation in this book meets standards 1—4 of the NCTM Guidelines:  1) Mathematics as Problem Solving
2) Mathematics as Communication  3) Mathematics as Reasoning  4) Mathematical Connections

# Corrrelation Chart

| Patterns and Functions | Algebra | Statistics | Probability | Geometry | Measurement |
|---|---|---|---|---|---|
| • | | • | | | • |
| • | | • | • | | • |
| • | | • | | • | • |
| • | • | • | • | | • |
| • | | | • | • | • |
| • | • | • | | • | • |
| • | | | | | • |
| • | | • | | | • |
| • | • | • | | | |
| • | • | • | | | |
| • | | • | | • | • |
| • | | | | • | • |
| • | | • | • | • | • |
| • | | • | | • | • |
| • | | • | | • | • |
| • | | • | | • | • |
| • | • | • | | • | • |
| | | • | | | • |
| | | • | | | • |
| • | | • | | | • |
| | | • | | | • |
| • | • | • | | • | • |
| • | | • | | • | • |
| • | • | • | • | | • |
| • | • | • | | • | • |
| • | | • | | | • |
| • | • | • | | | • |
| • | | • | | | |
| • | • | • | | | • |
| • | | • | | • | • |

9

# Time and Money

# A Year is...

**The Investigation:** Students explore non-traditional ways to describe a year.

**NCTM Connections:** computation • estimation • measurement • number sense

***Materials:*** calculators • Investigator's Log (p. 80) • Investigator's Wrap-Up (p. 81)

**Guide The Way**

⇨ Discuss traditional ways to describe a year: 365 days, 52 weeks, 12 months, etc. Then talk about how nontraditional equivalences might be obtained.

⇨ Help students brainstorm alternative ways to describe a year. To get them started, model a process for describing a year in terms of bread:

**BREAD/DAY**
breakfast—1 slice as toast
lunch—2 slices as sandwich
snack—2 slices
5 slices x 52 weeks = 260 slices/year
1 loaf = 28 slices
260 slices ÷ 28 slices = (9.29) approx. $9^1/_3$ loaves/year

⇨ Review the use of the calculator memory key, if necessary.

**Make The Connections**

⇨ Have students present and explain their findings. You might have peer partners verify each other's solutions.

⇨ Suggest ways to adjust calculations to reflect choices students make in real life. Refer to the model above. Point out that people usually don't have the same breakfast or lunch every day, and some days they might have no bread at all. Discuss how to reasonably account for such variations.

⇨ Invite students to acknowledge the class's findings for originality, creativity, humor, and accuracy.

⇨ Extend by having students investigate a year in the life of another family member, a pet, or an inanimate object.

# A Year is. . .

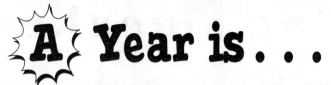

## The Investigation:
How many ways can you find to describe a year?

You could say that a year is 365 days or 12 months or 8,760 hours or 525,600 minutes. You could also say that it has 31,536,000 seconds.

But why stop here? A year is a lively thing, full of activity! A year might be 1,095 dog walks, or 20 yards of toothpaste. It could be 37 gallons of orange juice (or 4 ounces of prune juice). It could be 42 hours of waiting for the school bus.

What does a year mean to you?

**What To Do**

**1** Think of some creative ways to describe a year. Think of events you do weekly, daily, or many times a day. Consider what you do during the week that you *don't* do on weekends, or vice versa. Try to investigate ideas that nobody else will think of!

**2** Find ways to express your events. Can they be timed, counted, packaged, weighed, or measured in some other way?

**3** Figure out how often each event happens in a day, a week, or a month. Then find a total for the year. Use whatever unit fits your investigation.

**HINT:** Use your number sense and estimating skills. Adjust your calculations so they make sense.

**4** Prepare a list of what equals a year to you. Keep track of your calculations so you can explain and share your strategies.

**Share Your Findings**

**1** Make a class display of all the ways you found to describe a year. It could be a bulletin board, a poster, a card file, a slide show, or a skit.

**2** Tell how you came up with any descriptions that baffle your classmates!

# Buying Sneakers

**The Investigation:** Students explore the process of making a purchase to determine the total time it may take.

**NCTM Connections:** estimation • measurement • statistics • critical thinking

*Materials:* calculators • Investigator's Log (p. 80) • Investigator's Wrap-Up (p. 81)

➪ Discuss why people estimate how long something takes. Talk about meeting obligations, fitting tight schedules, or using time efficiently. Then discuss how people estimate the time it takes to complete a task. For instance, if the task involves travel, one should consider the distance involved, the method of transportation, traffic patterns, waiting time, and so on.

➪ Have students brainstorm to break down the shopping process into all its discrete parts. Remind students that the more precisely they can break down the task, the more accurate their final estimate is likely to be.

➪ If necessary, review computing with time values.

➪ Some students may benefit from a "dry run." If necessary, model a simpler purchasing task, such as buying a soft drink.

➪ Have students share their results and strategies. As a class, you might record all results in a line plot or tally table so students can see and discuss overall characteristics.

➪ Have students calculate the range of the estimates, as well as the mean, median, and mode. Challenge them to evaluate which of these measures most accurately describes the class results. Be aware that the most common response (mode) is not necessarily the most accurate. Encourage students to investigate outlying responses to determine what these estimates may reflect about the task.

➪ Discuss questions like these: *How can you verify the accuracy of estimates? Think about ways to speed up the shopping process. How could you save time next time—or could you? What do stores intentionally do to affect the speed of the shopping process? Why do they do these things?*

➪ Extend by having students who actually plan a sneaker- or shoe-buying spree to time each part of the task and share their findings with the class.

# Buying Sneakers

## The Investigation:
How long does it really take to buy a pair of sneakers?

You need a new pair of sneakers—today! How much time should you set aside for this shopping chore?

Buying anything takes time, maybe more than you think. A lot happens between the time when you decide to hit the mall and when you get home with your shoes. For example, it takes time to get from a parking space (or bus stop) to the store. It takes time for the clerk to notice you. Selecting a style you like takes time, too.

**What To Do**

**1** Assume that you have money to spend (thanks, Grandma!) on new sneakers. No need to include time for getting a job!

**2** Think of every part of the process of buying sneakers. List everything you do, from the moment you leave your home to the moment you return. Think about everything that happens at the store. Give an estimated time for each part of the process. Be realistic, not optimistic!

**3** Add up all the time estimates. Adjust your total, if necessary, so that it makes sense.

**4** Prepare to describe how you got your estimate.

**Share Your Findings**

**1** Share your estimate with classmates. Compare strategies.

**2** Based on class estimates, find the range of shopping times and the average shopping time.

**3** Discuss why estimates vary. Identify factors that help you evaluate the accuracy of an estimate, or decide that it's way off.

# Cash Comparison

**The Investigation:** Students examine and classify features of coins and bills.

**NCTM Connections:** money • logical reasoning • statistics

*Materials:* assorted coins and bills (or pictures of them) • hand lens • map or globe • Venn diagram (p. 86) • Investigator's Log (p. 80) • Investigator's Wrap-Up (p. 81)

**Guide The Way**

➪ Help students obtain an assortment of U.S. and foreign coins and bills to examine. Contact banks, coin shops, or private collectors. If this is not possible, ask your school or local library for books with pictures of coins and bills.

➪ Before students investigate foreign money, discuss common features found on all American money. Encourage students to look closely at the fronts and backs of the money to identify as many features as they can, and to describe them in mathematical terms, whenever possible. You might list features on the chalkboard to serve as an informal guide.

➪ Help students interpret words in languages they do not know. If necessary, remind them that a country's name will appear on its money in the language of that country, which may not be English. For instance, money that says *España* identifies its nation, Spain, in Spanish.

➪ Compare foreign exchange rates. Consult a newspaper's financial section for a table of values, which fluctuate daily with the activity of world financial markets. Challenge students to determine the value of ten American dollars in other currencies.

➪ Review the Venn diagram as a tool for comparing and contrasting. Invite students to design their own methods for presenting their findings, such as a gridded checklist or color-coordinated chart.

➪ Using a map or globe, have students locate the countries from which the money they examine comes.

**Make The Connections**

➪ Have students present their findings. You might compile common features on one large chart.

➪ Discuss questions such as these: *What features identify the front and back of a coin or bill? Does money from neighboring nations share more similarities than money from distant countries? Does the size of a coin or bill reflect its value?* Use examples from the money you investigated to support your answer.

➪ Extend by having students design an original coin or bill. It should display characteristics found on most money, but may introduce new symbols or include new features.

# Cash Comparison

**The Investigation:**
What features are shared by money of many countries?

You know what money is and what it's used for. And you probably know that each nation has its own money. You know that you can't pay for pizza in Paris with *pesos*, and that yogurt in Yokohama costs *yen*.

Despite its name, shape, or design, all money shares common features. Use your investigative skills to find similarities in coins and bills of the world.

**What To Do**

**1** Get an assortment of coins and bills from many countries, or pictures of them. Decide whether to examine all coins, all bills, or some of each. Get a hand lens to help you see small details.

**2** Analyze money from 4 or more countries, including the United States. Think of features to look for on all of the money. Observe closely. Think of ways to sort and classify what you see. Think about what it means and why it's there.

**3** Prepare a diagram, a chart, a checklist, or other visual display to organize your findings based on the money you examine.

**HINT:** Use a Venn diagram to to show common features and distinct elements.

**Share Your Findings**

**1** Summarize what you discovered. Describe features *common* to all of the money you analyzed. Describe special features *unique* to certain kinds of money.

**2** Discuss features you don't understand. Brainstorm ways to learn more about them.

**3** Use a map or globe to match each type of money with the country where it is used.

# Line of Fries

**The Investigation:** Students explore data about french fries in order to represent yearly sales in a unique way.

**NCTM Connections:** computation • estimation • measurement • proportional reasoning

*Materials:* calculators • road atlas • Letter Shell (p. 87) • Investigator's Log (p. 80) • Investigator's Wrap-Up (p. 81)

➪ Highlight creative marketing techniques by discussing how some restaurants publicize how many of a certain food item they've sold over time. Ask students to explain whether they think this strategy is effective.

➪ Point out that this investigation becomes more manageable when students figure out how to break it down into small steps. Encourage them to prepare a plan for tracking sales of french fries, and then consider which restaurants they might approach for data.

➪ Have students prepare a letter of introduction to the restaurant manager before visiting. The letter should briefly describe the investigation and tell how the results will be used.

➪ Encourage different students to gather data from different types of restaurants so that results can be compared.

➪ Provide a road atlas. As needed, review how to read and use the map scale.

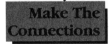

➪ Have students present their findings and explain how they figured them out. You might have pairs verify each other's solutions.

➪ Have students create a class display of their french fry statements. Invite students to tell which statements they think are the most inventive.

➪ Extend by having students estimate the length of a line of fries the class eats in one year. You may also want to compare the class line of french fries to a healthier line of perhaps carrots, beans, or asparagus. Discuss what you find.

➪ Extend by having the class figure out the weight or volume of some foods they eat in a year. For example, they can determine the number of bathtubs of soda they drink or bowling-ball weights of ice cream they eat!

# Line of Fries

**The Investigation:**
How can you describe a year's sales of french fries?

How long is a line of fries that stretches from Dallas to Detroit? *Who cares?* Fast-food restaurant owners, that's who!

If you could figure out the length of a line of ALL the fries a restaurant sells in a year, you'd have a clever advertising idea. It's an idea that could interest the owner of your favorite fast-food joint!

Enter the creative world of marketing. Develop a catchy way to tell customers how many french fries your client sells in a year.

**What To Do**

**1** Visit a local fast-food restaurant. Interview the manager to find out how many orders of french fries they sell. Use whatever sales data you can get—daily, weekly, or quarterly sales, pounds of potatoes, and so on.

**2** Estimate about how many fries are in one order. Also estimate the length of a typical fry. Or, chip in with friends and buy an order of fries to get more accurate hands-on (and mouth-on!) knowledge of this data.

**3** Use your findings about the number of and size of french fry orders to estimate how many fries the restaurant sells in one year.

**HINT:**
Be creative! A line of fries that climbs Mount Everest and back down is more engaging to read about than one that stretches from Oak Park to Evansville.

**4** Calculate the length of the line *ALL* the fries would make if placed end to end.

**5** Once you've figured out your french fry mileage, consult a road atlas. Use it to help you make a statement that describes the number of fries sold as a distance people will understand. You might use the mileage between where you live and a familiar city or well-known vacation spot.

**Share Your Findings**

**1** Present your ad idea to the class. Try presenting a poster, newspaper ad, banner, or press release. Show it to the restaurant manager.

**2** Explain to classmates your process of coming up with your ad idea.

# Party Sampler

**The Investigation:** Students explore all the elements of catering a big party.

**NCTM Connections:** sampling • proportional reasoning • estimation • measurement • computation

***Materials:*** assorted take-out menus and store flyers • tally table (p. 85) • calculators • Investigator's Log (p. 80) • Investigator's Wrap-Up (p. 81)

**Guide The Way**

⇨ Discuss the process of sampling. Describe how sensible decisions can be made based on data from representative samples.

⇨ Help students learn to think like caterers. Encourage them to create questionnaires that will elicit responses from potential clients about their catering needs for a specific event.

⇨ Have different students investigate catering parties for different size groups. For example, students can plan a class party, a grade party, a middle school party, or one for the entire school.

⇨ Provide take-out menus and store flyers to help students determine costs. If you know someone who does professional catering, you might invite that person to talk to the class about party-planning pointers and pitfalls.

⇨ As needed, review how to write and solve proportions.

**Make The Connections**

⇨ When students present their findings, guide them to explain how they used data from the samples to make purchasing decisions. Have them explain how they calculated total cost and per-person cost.

⇨ Extend by having students investigate the cost of catering a large sit-down dinner to celebrate a special occasion, such as a birthday, a graduation, or a holiday. The dinner should have a balanced and nutritious menu.

# Party Sampler

## The Investigation:
What do you have to do to plan a large party?

You want to throw a party for your whole school, with lots to eat and drink. A caterer would be a big help. But caterers are expensive. Plus, they have silly names like Party Thyme, The Perfect Plum, and Kitchen Coup. Yecchh! So *you* plan it all. Put on your chef's thinking hat, get a pencil, and get busy. Party on!

**What To Do**

**1** List possible foods and drinks to serve at a big party. Use your list to make a questionnaire about what to serve. Poll a sampling of students from different grades to learn what party foods and drinks they like. Also find out how much of each they'd eat. For example, kids who pick pizza can tell how many slices they usually have.

**2** Use the results from the questionnaires to determine which party foods and drinks to serve. Also decide how much of everything to buy, bake, or prepare. Use take-out menus or cookbooks, or visit stores to estimate what all the food and drink will cost.

**3** Figure out the non-food items you'll need—plates, cups, napkins, and so on. Think of what else you need for serving, decorating, or cleaning up. Decide how and where to get the items. Do research to estimate costs.

**4** As any caterer would do, prepare a party proposal. List everything you need for the party and the total estimated cost. Give a per-student cost, too.

**HINT:** Food is expensive. You need enough to satisfy your guests, but not so much that it goes to waste.

**Share Your Findings**

**1** Display or distribute copies of your proposal. Tell how you reached your conclusions about food preferences and quantities, and how you figured costs. Discuss the snags you encountered, and how you dealt with them.

**21**

# Home for Sale

**The Investigation:** Students explore ways to quantify information about their own home.

**NCTM Connections:** computation • estimation • measurement • geometry

*Materials:* classified ads from local newspapers or realtors
• assorted measuring tools • calculators • grid paper (pp. 82-83)
• Investigator's Log (p. 80) • Investigator's Wrap-Up (p. 81)

**Guide The Way**

⇨ Talk about the kinds of data typically found in a For Sale ad for a house or apartment, and why it's there. You might put some representative ads on the overhead projector to stimulate class discussion.

⇨ Encourage students to think of unique ways to quantify information about their homes. They might start with an inventory of the number of windows, doors, rooms, or closets, then progress to other mathematical descriptions, such as area, surface area, volume, or weight. Students can focus on individual features or on relationships among features.

⇨ Have students describe their home in as many mathematical ways as they can. Remind them to label all measurements with the proper unit, such as square feet or cubic centimeters.

⇨ It might help students to sketch a floor plan of their home (or parts of it) on grid paper, and then record measurements where they belong.

⇨ Review how to find the area of irregular figures and the volume of rectangular solids, if necessary. Review using the calculator memory key.

**Make The Connections**

⇨ Have students present their ads and any accompanying illustrations they may have made. Peer partners might verify each other's calculations.

⇨ Suggest ways to evaluate the ads. Students might judge them for originality, precision, variety, or usefulness.

⇨ Extend by having students develop interesting mathematical data about their neighborhood, school, classroom, or a well-known public facility.

# Home for Sale

## The Investigation:
What mathematical ways are there to describe your home?

Most Home For Sale ads in the newspaper describe houses or apartments by number of rooms, area, features, and cost. How ordinary! You can do better. Use your mathematical skills to create a precise, interesting, and unique Home For Sale ad.

### What To Do

**1** Read some Home For Sale ads in the classified section of your local newspaper to learn how they describe houses or apartments. Get a feel for what people say about a place to grab the attention of possible buyers.

**2** Now, imagine putting your home up for sale. First, figure out how to describe it in ordinary terms. Then use your creativity and imagination to describe it mathematically. For instance, you might find the area of all the windows. You might find the volume of all kitchen cupboards, or the surface area of all built-in counters. Or, give the average distance between outlets or average number of hangers the closets can hold. Be clever! Be wild! Be mathematical!

**3** Now, get really outrageous. Create humorous extra descriptions of your home, such as "Enough doorknobs to hang up 2 dozen T-shirts without ever opening a drawer."

**4** Prepare a For Sale ad that makes your home sound uniquely and mathematically appealing.

### Share Your Findings

**1** Display your Home For Sale ad. Explain how you determined the data you chose to present.

**2** Read other people's ads to see which ones appeal to you. Evaluate them by asking yourself questions like these: *Which ads might attract serious buyers? Which might attract big families? Which give the most unexpected data? Which most impress your math teacher?*

# Classified Information

**The Investigation:** Students explore costs of placing classified ads in newspapers.

**NCTM Connections:** computation • estimation • measurement

***Materials:*** newspapers • grid paper (pp. 82-83) • calculators • Investigator's Log (p. 80) • Investigator's Wrap-Up (p. 81)

**Guide The Way**

⇨ Have students look through the classified sections of newspapers to learn the difference between general ads and classified ads. Guide them to notice recurring features, such as commonly used abbreviations, use of statistics, facts, or slogans, and identifying information.

⇨ Have students create a classified ad they'd like to place. Help them find information to help them determine the cost of placing the ad. Some papers publish this information in the classified section; others have an advertising department that will provide the information.

⇨ Discuss the meaning of the term *column inch*, and how to apply this idea to the cost of a classified ad.

⇨ As students compare the costs of placing an ad in different newspapers, discuss options, such as placing a big ad once vs. placing a smaller ad several times, or placing ads in more than one paper. Invite students to give their opinions on which options make the most sense, and why.

**Make The Connections**

⇨ Have students present their ads, their plans for placing them, and the reasons for their decisions.

⇨ Have students evaluate ads for effectiveness. For example, ask students whether they think that more costly ads are always more effective.

⇨ Suggest ways to evaluate the advantages and disadvantages of choosing one newspaper over another. For instance, ask: *Do some papers have a larger circulation? Do any have special sections where an ad would be more prominent? Do any attract certain kinds of readers?*

⇨ Extend by having students investigate the costs of placing a similar ad on local radio or television. Have them compare the costs and the effects of placing the ad on a broadcast medium vs. a print medium.

# Classified Information

## The Investigation:
How much does it cost to place an ad in the newspaper?

Classified ads come in all sizes. Some are tiny ones that appear at the end of a column of text. Others take up an entire page or part of it. Some include art or photos. What determines how much an ad costs? Well, that depends. In this investigation, you can find out.

**What To Do**

**1** Look through some newspapers and magazines to see different kinds of classified ads. Notice size and shape, art, position on the page, and layout.

**2** Think of something you'd like to advertise—an item to sell, a service to offer, or your own business.

**3** Plan an ad with the information you want to include. If you want art, make a sketch or prepare a piece of computer clip art. You can always rework your idea once you learn more details about placing an ad.

**4** Research the cost of placing your ad in 3 different newspapers. Prepare by listing questions to ask, such as: *How does the size of an ad affect cost? Does an ad with art cost more than an ad with only words? Do costs vary depending on when or where the ad appears, or how many times it appears?*

**5** Assume you have an ad budget of $300. Decide the best way to spend it, based on the data you get. Pick the paper, the location and style of the ad, and when and how often it will appear.

**HINT:**
The cost of placing an ad may rely on a unit called a column inch. Find out what this means.

**6** Write the complete ad, including art, if needed. Calculate its cost.

**Share Your Findings**

**1** Present your final ad to classmates. Give a summary of how you chose to spend your ad budget. Invite and answer questions classmates may ask.

**2** Describe the factors that influenced your decision, such as the circulation of the paper, the kind of people who'll read it, and its cost.

# On-Air Analysis

**The Investigation:** Students observe, classify, and analyze television commercials.

**NCTM Connections:** statistics • logical reasoning • percents and fractions

*Materials:* tally table (p. 85) • grid paper (pp. 82-83) • circle graph (p. 84) • protractor • Investigator's Log (p. 80) • Investigator's Wrap-Up (p. 81)

**Guide The Way**

⇨ Discuss factors that influence television advertising decisions. Talk about data advertisers might use to decide when to schedule certain commercials.

⇨ Alert students that commercials typically air in clusters, and may be brief and distracting. Talk about ways to focus on the task. Encourage students to use a VCR to help them with this investigation.

⇨ As needed, help students group the different kinds of products advertised into reasonable categories. Encourage them to think of broad groupings.

⇨ You may wish to assign particular time slots to different students to ensure a broader sampling of advertising data.

⇨ Review how to construct a circle graph. Also review the relationship between fractions and percents.

**Make The Connections**

⇨ Have students display their graphs, present their findings, and explain how they determined their categories. Have students who made circle graphs explain how they determined the size of each sector.

⇨ Invite students to describe any trends or surprises in their own data and in the data classmates found. Ask them to generalize, if possible, about the kinds of commercials shown during the hours watched.

⇨ Extend by having students investigate ways to categorize commercials other than by kinds of products advertised. Examples might include animated vs. live action, more (or less) than 30 seconds, and so on.

⇨ Challenge students to record the amount of time per hour devoted to commercials, public service announcements, trailers for upcoming shows, news breaks, station identification, and the main program itself. Have them make a circle graph to show this data.

Name: _____  Date: _____

# On-Air Analysis

## The Investigation:
What kinds of products do TV advertisers want *you* to buy?

If you described your TV viewing habits, you'd probably mention the shows you like. Advertisers, the people who pay for your programs, would rather know that you're watching their commercials. Without commercials, there'd be no sit-coms, no talk shows, no MTV! TV shows that don't sell products don't stay on the air.

So what kinds of commercials air during your favorite shows? How can you categorize them? Which products are advertised most often? Are the same products shown at night as during the day? Find out by analyzing the ads.

**What To Do**

**1** Brainstorm a list all the kinds of products you see advertised on TV.

**2** Develop several categories from your list, such as car/truck ads, ads for clothes, fast food, sports equipment, and so on. Create a tally table using your categories.

**3** Pick a 1-hour TV time slot. Choose one channel to watch for the entire hour. Carefully tally EVERY commercial you see. If an ad airs more than once, tally it each time.

**4** With your completed tally table, create a bar or circle graph to display your findings. Your graph should show the kinds of commercials that aired and how many of each appeared during the hour you watched.

**5** Use percents or fractions to describe your data mathematically.

**HINT:** Using a VCR can make your tallying job easier.

**Share Your Findings**

**1** Tell how you developed your categories. Explain what you did when you saw a commercial that didn't fit one of your categories.

**2** Present your tables and graphs. Summarize the data shown by answering questions like these: *How many commercials were shown per hour? Which kinds of products were advertised most/least often? Were any commercials repeated? How often?* Develop other questions classmates can answer, based on their on-air analyses.

# Inflation Summation

**The Investigation:** Students explore how prices of everyday items have changed over time.

**NCTM Connections:** percents and fractions • statistics • number sense • estimation

*Materials:* calculators • letter shell (p. 87) • grid paper (pp. 82-83) • Investigator's Log (p. 80) • Investigator's Wrap-Up (p.81)

**Guide The Way**

⇨ Discuss the concept of inflation. Ask students whether they think all prices rise over time. Talk about why some things rise dramatically in price, others rise more gradually, and still others stay the same or decrease in price.

⇨ Guide students to choose items to research for which past prices will be relatively easy to obtain. Such items include household staples, such as bread, milk, eggs, or lettuce, or supplies, such as toothpaste, soap, or toilet paper. People often recall common entertainment costs over the years, such as the price of movie admission or of a newspaper. Students can use the Letter Shell to help them draft letters of request for information.

⇨ As needed, review how to find what percent one number is of another, and to calculate the percent of increase and decrease.

⇨ Talk about the advantages of using line graphs to display the data students will gather.

**Make The Connections**

⇨ After students present their findings, have them compare and contrast all the data and predictions.

⇨ Help students summarize their discoveries by posing questions like these: *What general statement can you make, if any, about the changes in prices of everyday items? What patterns, if any, emerge? Which kinds of things seem to rise in price most dramatically? Why do you think they do? Which rise in price more gradually? Explain why. What kinds of things stay the same or decrease in price? How can this be?*

⇨ Extend by inviting an expert to address the class with more specific data and background to explain the cost history of particular items, such as computers, cars, jeans, or watches.

# Inflation Summation

## The Investigation:
How do the prices of things change over time?

As a rule, don't go shopping with someone who's been in a remote cave for the last 50 years or so. That's because the cost of most things has risen dramatically over the years. Your friend may suffer sticker shock over today's prices!

The prices of everyday items change over time. But do bread, milk, pizza, and ice cream prices rise at the same rate as those of magazines, stamps, and back packs? What kinds of things have increased the most in price? Which have changed the least? Investigate to find out.

**What To Do**

**1** Choose five items you or your family buys regularly. Record the typical price of each item in a table.

**2** Find out what these same items cost 10, 20, and 30 years ago and, if possible, even further in the past. Interview parents and elders to gather this data, then add it to your table. Speak with several people to verify past prices. Visit the library, contact city, state, or federal agencies, or write to the producers of the products. On-line research may also help.

**3** Prepare a line graph to show the data. Write a summary of your findings in which you analyze the price changes for your items over time. Use percents or fractions to describe these changes.

**4** Based on your data, predict what your items might cost in the years 2000, 2010, and 2020. Extend your graph to show this information.

**HINT:** To display your data, make five separate line graphs, or create a color code to distinguish among five lines on a single graph.

**Share Your Findings**

**1** Display your graph(s) and present your findings. Tell how you got your data.

**2** Explain how you used mathematics to analyze the changes in prices. Talk about trends you noticed. Describe any surprises your research revealed.

**3** Explain how you made your predictions for future prices.

# Creating an Impression

**The Investigation:** Students explore ways to construct or vary graphs to convey different visual impressions of the data.

**NCTM Connections:** • statistics • number sense • patterns and functions

***Materials:*** newspapers and magazines • sample graphs (p. 32)
• grid paper (pp. 82-83) • Investigator's Log (p. 80) • Investigator's Wrap-Up (p. 81)

**Guide The Way**

➪ Duplicate and distribute page 32 to help students understand the concept of misleading graphs. Discuss the idea that graphs can be used to create certain visual impressions, and that these impressions may be meant to mislead. Talk about who might make use of this tactic.

➪ Help students understand that the second bar graph on page 32 misleads by giving the visual impression that chocolate is preferred 3 to 1, although the data shows that 12 people preferred chocolate and 8 chose vanilla (3:2). Be sure students recognize that beginning the vertical scale at 6 rather than at 0 can give accurate data a misleading appearance.

➪ Talk about how the two line graphs show the same data, but give different visual impressions. Discuss how adjusting the horizontal spacing of the scale changes the appearance of the growth data.

➪ Invite students to suggest ways, other than adjusting scales to put a particular spin on the graphed data. For instance, varying the width of bars on the same graph changes their impression, though not their value.

➪ If possible, obtain copies of *USA Today* and various news magazines, which are good sources for simple graphs.

**Make The Connections**

➪ When students present their graphs, have them explain the effects of their changes on the appearance of the data. Invite others to suggest different ways to alter the appearance.

➪ Extend by having students investigate how measures of average—mean, median, and mode—can be used in misleading ways. Give the example of a student who boasts that his test average is 96, based on scores of 59, 96, 62, 70, and 96. In this case, the *mode* is 96, but the *mean* is 76.6 and the *median* is 70. Challenge students to create other examples of intentionally poor applications of these measures of central tendency.

# Creating an Impression

## The Investigation:
How can graphs be visually misleading?

You can put a slant on data by the way you display it. Advertisers do this. So do *spin doctors* who work for politicians. They present data to give the particular visual impression they want to convey.

You too can manipulate the appearance of data by the way you construct a graph of that data.

**What To Do**

**1** Examine the bar graphs and line graphs on page 32. In each case, the graphs present the same data, yet convey different impressions by how they are made. Answer the questions to see how a spin doctor may have manipulated the graphs.

**2** Now you're on your own. Look through magazines and newspapers for a graph that interests you. Cut out the graph. Study it closely to understand the information it presents. What impression does the data give?

**3** **WITHOUT CHANGING ANY DATA**, rework the graph so that it gives a different visual impression. Title and label your revised graph.

**4** Make a poster that displays the two graphs side by side. Give your poster a catchy headline to suggest the different impressions the two graphs give.

**5** Be ready to explain what you did to change the visual impression of the original graph. Write a description of how your new graph presents the data in a different light.

HINT: Think about how adjusting one of the scales gives the data a new slant.

**Share Your Findings**

**1** Display your poster and share your description. Discuss the data the original graph gives and the impression it creates. Then highlight the changes in your revised graph. Explain what you did to create a new spin.

**2** Invite classmates to suggest other ways to create a different impression of that same data.

# Creating an Impression

**These two graphs show ice cream preferences of 20 8th graders.**

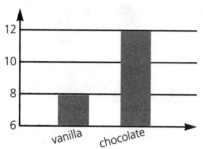
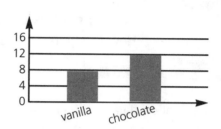

Look at the bar graphs that show ice cream preferences. Each presents exactly the same data, yet the way each is constructed gives a different impression.

Which graph misleads? _____

In what way does it do this? _____

_____

_____

_____

**These two graphs show how the money in Stoyan's account grew over four months.**

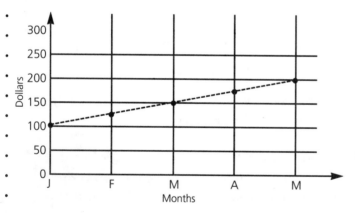
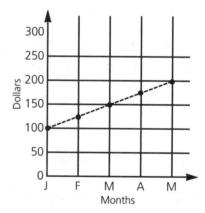

Compare the line graphs that show growth rates. Both show the exact same data, yet they convey very different impressions.

Describe the impression each graph gives. How do they give different messages?

_____

_____

_____

_____

# Size and Shape

# Eggs-amination

**The Investigation:** Students explore differences in egg sizes.

**NCTM Connections:** measurement • statistics • patterns and relationships

**Materials:** assorted measurement tools • eggs of different size designations • small cups or bowls • paper towels • grid paper (pp. 82-83) • letter shell (p. 87) • Investigator's Log (p. 80) • Investigator's Wrap-Up (p. 81)

**Guide The Way**

⇨ Help students name the different size designations customarily used to describe eggs. Discuss what students think those designations mean. Talk about problems caused by size descriptions that are not clear.

⇨ Help students obtain a variety of eggs of different sizes. Talk about ways to measure the eggs. Ideas include finding the circumference (vertically or horizontally), weight (with or without the shell), volume (of raw egg), length, and width. Guide students to identify the kind of measuring tool most suitable for finding each measure. Provide containers, paper towels, spoons, and other tools to facilitate the investigation.

⇨ As students investigate egg sizes, they'll notice variations between and within each category. Discuss the concept of range, as needed.

⇨ Help students determine ways to record their information in graphs, tables, or charts.

⇨ Students may want to investigate distinctions between raw and cooked eggs. If so, you might have them bring in hard-boiled eggs of different sizes. Or, set up a hot plate in the classroom to boil the eggs on site.

**Make The Connections**

⇨ Have students present their findings and explain how they figured them out. You might have students combine their results into a class chart from which they can make inferences and draw conclusions. Discuss questions like these: *Are all eggs in a size category really the same size? Is there overlap between sizes? Are all eggs in one carton the same size? How much variation is there?*

⇨ Have students contact the U.S. Department of Agriculture, the American Egg Board (1460 Renaissance Drive, Park Ridge, IL 60068), or a local farmer to learn the rules about egg sizes and to compare their findings with the official designations.

⇨ Extend by having students investigate variations in the sizes of other "standard" foods, such as fruits, vegetables, or cookies.

# Eggs-amination

## The Investigation:
How many ways can you find to describe and compare eggs?

Some people call eggs a perfect food. They're cheap, nutritious, easy to cook, and tasty. But egg descriptions aren't always perfect. Eggs are sorted by size into vague categories like jumbo, extra large, or large. If you had a mystery egg, would you know its size? Why, it's enough to scramble your brain!

What distinguishes a medium egg from an extra large one? Are all jumbo eggs the same size? Be a hard-boiled math investigator and find out!

**What To Do**

**1** Bring in some raw eggs from home. Make sure to get eggs of different sizes. Label them in some way to remind you which is which.

**2** Brainstorm ways to measure and compare egg sizes. Use different measurement tools: scale, tape measure, ruler, measuring cups, and so on.

**3** Make a plan for measuring, comparing, and analyzing different egg sizes. You may want to break an egg or two. (If so, get some small cups or bowls.) Be sure to clean up—and enjoy a big omelet!

**4** Conduct your investigation. Record data, using exact units of weight, volume, length, or any other measurement you use.

**HINT:** Are eggs the same size whether raw or cooked? How can you find out?

**5** Based on your findings, prepare a report of what you learned about the size categories of eggs. Include a chart, graph, or other visual aid to help others understand your findings.

**Share Your Findings**

**1** Present your results to the class. Be specific about what you did, how you did it, what you found out, and what you didn't learn.

**2** Discuss whether your results match the results others found. If so, what conclusions can you make about egg sizes? If not, what can you conclude?

# Package Deal

**The Investigation:** Students explore the issues that influence package designs; they design and create their own package for a small object.

**NCTM Connections:** spatial reasoning • geometry • estimation • measurement

*Materials:* grid paper (pp. 82-83) • measurement tools • letter shell (p. 87) • Investigator's Log (p. 80) • Investigator's Wrap-Up (p. 81)

**Guide The Way**

➩ Invite students to visit a supermarket or department store to notice the array of packaging used to protect and display products. Or, bring in an assortment of products in varied packaging for them to examine in class.

➩ As students discuss the different kinds of packages, guide them to address manufacturers' concerns, such as safety during shipping and handling, "stackability," cost-efficient use of materials, or adequate space for product information. Suggest that students also consider marketing issues, such as how a package opens (and closes) or whether its contents should be visible.

➩ Have each student bring in a small, unpackaged item from home. Facilitate a class swap of the items. Explain to students that the object they get must be packaged safely so it could be shipped, stored, and displayed in a store. Be sure students realize that they will get their own item back at the end of the investigation.

➩ Encourage students to use a hands-on approach to drawing the unfolded patterns for their three-dimensional packages. As needed, review the properties of polyhedrons and other space figures and how to make two-dimensional patterns for them. It may help some students to take apart a box or other container to better visualize how to create a flat pattern for it.

**Make The Connections**

➩ As students share and discuss their package designs, guide them to address the idea that effective packaging meets the needs of the consumer, the manufacturer, and the store owner.

➩ If possible, invite a designer to address the class about packaging issues.

➩ Extend by inviting students to send their completed designs and explanations to manufacturers to get feedback on their ideas.

# Package Deal

## The Investigation:
How do you decide the best shape and size package for a product?

Why doesn't cereal come in pyramid-shaped boxes? Why isn't steak packed in tubes? What *are* the best shapes used to package the stuff you buy? What are the best sizes? Think like a manufacturer to understand packaging choices.

Don't come apart or collapse. Just start packing—for this investigation!

**What To Do**

**1** Brainstorm a list of shapes and sizes of packages you see in stores. Consider the information packages give. Think of what's inside, other than the product itself. Consider how packages open and close.

**2** Discuss why manufacturers choose these shapes and sizes. Give the advantages of each package for its product. Imagine manufacturers' *real* concerns, such as cost, materials, safety, and stackability.

**3** Bring in an unpackaged object from home. Swap it with a classmate.

**4** Plan an effective package for the object. Account for any space needed inside. Decide whether the object should be seen and if so, how to do this. Plan how to open the package (and close it, if needed).

**5** Draw and label the unfolded pattern for your package. Show what appears on each surface of the package.

**6** Make your package or a final sketch of it. Give all dimensions. Write an explanation of the shape, size, and features you used.

**HINT:** Fold your pattern to make sure it works. Check that product information appears where and how you want it.

**Share Your Findings**

**1** Display the model or drawing of your package and the pattern for it. Share your explanations of the features you included.

**2** Explain why your package is right for your product. Describe how you used your spatial sense, estimating, and measuring skills in your design.

# Composite Car

**The Investigation:** Students analyze car features to determine the characteristics that comprise the "typical" car in your area.

**NCTM Connections:** statistics • logical reasoning • patterns • probability

*Materials:* tally table (p. 85) • Investigator's Log (p. 80) • Investigator's Wrap-Up (p. 81)

**Guide The Way**

⇨ Discuss car characteristics that people can choose, such as make, model, size, color, and options. Steer students away from specific makes (Ford, Honda, Volkswagen, etc.) to focus on generic features, such as type (i.e., sport utility vehicle, convertible), size (i.e., subcompact, mid-size), and options (i.e., roof rack, fog lights).

⇨ Help students create a way to compile data about cars. They might make a checklist or tally table in which to record data based on their observations.

⇨ Talk about safe plans and locations for gathering data. For instance, student teams might canvass the parking lot at a local mall or supermarket. They might pick a well-trafficked intersection and gather data on cars as they stop. They could wait in a bus shelter on the side of a road to tally cars that pass.

⇨ After students have gathered data, they may or may not see emerging patterns. If they need additional data, encourage them to collect more auto data over more days. Or, students might merge their data.

⇨ If needed, review the meaning of *mode*, the measure of central tendency that identifies the trait occurring most frequently. In this investigation, the composite car should reflect the mode of each group of data.

⇨ Students should sketch their composite car so that it presents typical features based on the research. They should describe characteristics that may be difficult to draw, such as antilock brakes or "is a foreign car."

**Make The Connections**

⇨ Have students present their findings and drawings and explain how they made their decisions. You might have them display the drawings with labels or other written information on a bulletin board.

⇨ Invite a local car dealer to address the class about features he or she sees in demand recently. Students can prepare questions to ask the dealer, including his or her response to their analysis.

⇨ Extend by having students conduct an on-line car analysis with students in other parts of the country. They can post their survey forms for "remote data collectors"— students in other areas who can do similar research.

# Composite Car

### The Investigation:
What features describe the typical car in your area?

Americans love cars. And they love their choice of models, colors, and features. Given the range of autos in your area, what's a *typical* car? How can you figure this out? And who'd be most interested in knowing this information? You can conduct an auto analysis to find out.

**What To Do**

**1** Brainstorm a list of car styles (sedan, hatchback, etc.), features (2 doors, moon roof, etc.), and typical details (color, foreign vs. domestic, etc.) Use your list to create a form you can use to gather data about cars in your area.

**2** Plan to do research over several days. Find ways and locations to tally information about cars. You might look at cars in a parking lot or tally cars that halt at a certain stop light.

**3** Look at the data you collect. Draw conclusions about what features are most typical in your area. Use the data to draw and describe a "composite" car. Such a car may or may not really exist, but it would have the most common features you observed.

**HINT:**
Be sure to see a range of cars, not just new cars at an auto showroom.

**Share Your Findings**

**1** Display your composite car. Tell how you determined its details and features. You can explain hard-to-draw details, such as "over 3 years old."

**2** Compare and contrast your composite car with the cars other students created. Talk about the variations in these "models."

# Tile in Style

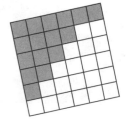

**The Investigation:** Students explore the process of tiling a floor.

**NCTM Connections:** proportional and visual reasoning
• geometry • measurement • percent

*Materials:* grid paper (pp. 82-83)
• Investigator's Log (p. 80) • Investigator's Wrap-Up (p. 81)

**Guide The Way**

⇨ Encourage students to look at tiled floors to see how the tile is laid. Provide pictures of different tile designs. If there's a tile store in your area, invite students to visit it to see several real-life examples in one place.

⇨ Review how to make a scale model on grid paper. Advise students to consider the size of tile they've selected when choosing their scale.

⇨ Some students may prefer to work with paper cut-outs to plan their designs. If so, these students can cut out squares and half squares (rectangles or triangles) to visualize how their floor will look.

⇨ Discuss the advantages of starting tiling in corners, in the middle of a floor, or in places where whole tiles can be readily placed.

⇨ In reality, tile setters must allow space between tiles for grout. For this investigation, allow students to ignore this issue. Let them assume that the size of the tile includes space for grout.

**Make The Connections**

⇨ Have students present their floor plans and tell how they worked them out.

⇨ If you have the equipment, you might make transparencies of students' floor plans for use with an overhead projector.

⇨ If possible, invite a tile setter to address the class on issues involved in tiling a room. He or she can evaluate students' designs and make suggestions.

⇨ Extend by having students investigate the actual cost of tiles for their room based on their plan and on Dave's "10% rule."

# Tile in Style

### The Investigation:
How do you tile a floor?

Tiles come in many shapes and sizes. Yet tile setters still face the same problems they've faced for centuries—where in the room to begin, where to end, how to tile around obstacles, and how to fit tiles in an area that won't hold an exact number of them.

Imagine that *you* are responsible for tiling the floor of a room in your home. How will you do it? No need to call Dave's Tile Company. Start with a floor plan and a careful design.

**What To Do**

**1** Choose a room in your home. Choose <u>one</u> size of square tile for the floor. Use 6-inch, 8-inch, 12-inch, or 14-inch tiles. You may use two colors of the same size tile if you want to make a design.

**2** Draw a scale model of the floor on grid paper. Make extra copies—laying tile takes planning. As experienced workers say, "Measure twice, cut once."

**3** Use the scale drawing to design your tile pattern. Begin by deciding whether to tile "on a square" or "on a diagonal." Then decide where to start: on one end, in the middle, or along one side. Tiles can be cut.

**4** Prepare a final sketch of your tiled floor. Color it if you used two colors of tile. Provide all dimensions, the scale used, and the number of tiles you'll need.

**5** Now that you have your tile plan, plan a tile order. Dave says that smart tile setters always order 10% more tiles to allow for breakage.

**HINT:**
You can tile around things, under them, or do some of both. Although some objects may be hard to move, a level floor is important.

**Share Your Findings**

**1** Display your final design and point out all the information it shows.

**2** Describe the difficulties you faced in making your design. Explain how you solved these problems. Tell what you might do differently next time.

# Play Space

**The Investigation:** Students explore the characteristics of a good outdoor playground and design their own.

**NCTM Connections:** geometry • estimation • measurement • proportional reasoning • statistics

*Materials:* tally table (p. 85) • grid paper (pp. 82-83) • measuring tools • Investigator's Log (p. 80) • Investigator's Wrap-Up (p. 81)

**Guide The Way**

➪ Discuss the major features of outdoor playground spaces. Guide students to recognize the importance of variety, age-appropriate equipment, durability, and a convenient layout. Also point out the necessity of safety and comfort features, such as benches, shade, fencing, ground cover, and so on.

➪ Help students design and conduct a survey of playground preferences. They will use the data they gather to help them create their own playground plan. If there are popular playgrounds in your area, you might plan trips there so students can examine, evaluate, sketch, and measure them. Point out safety and comfort features (or lack of them).

➪ If necessary, review the concepts of scale drawing and area.

**Make The Connections**

➪ Have students present their plans and explain the process they used to design their playgrounds. You might have peer partners verify each other's plans to check that they meet the guidelines.

➪ Invite students to compare and contrast the playgrounds they designed. You might have them select and combine the best features of many plans into one terrific design.

➪ Extend by having students investigate the approximate cost of constructing the playground they designed. They could check equipment catalogs or talk to contractors, architects, or the school property and grounds manager.

Name: _____  Date: _____

# Play Space

## The Investigation:
What does it take to design an outdoor play space?

You've been to playgrounds. You've soared on swings or relaxed on wide benches. But did you ever wonder why the playground is arranged as it is? After all, it didn't just pop up. People planned each and every feature.

You might do better! After all, as a former little kid, you know what kids like. Apply your unique understanding to this mathematical investigation.

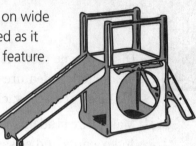

**What To Do**

**1** Think of important features for a playground. Include equipment that offers variety for kids of many ages. Remember safety features, places for adults, boundaries, and comfort features, such as benches.

**2** Conduct a survey in your school to identify the playground equipment kids want most. Ask which safety and comfort features kids value.

**3** Use your data to plan a new playground in a rectangular space 80 feet long by 60 feet wide. Arrange it as you like, but include at least four different kinds of equipment. Account for safety and comfort.

**HINT:** Overestimate the area you need for each kind of equipment to allow enough space for it and for safe space around it.

**4** Plan your space on grid paper. Determine a sensible scale. Label everything in your plan. Be flexible—you may have to adjust the size of equipment to make everything fit.

**5** Show a draft of your plan to classmates. Revise based on their comments.

**Share Your Findings**

**1** Display your playground plan. Talk about how you made your various decisions.

**2** Compare and contrast your playground plan with the plans others made. What unique ideas did some students offer? Is there a way to revise your plan to include other good ideas?

# Tower Power

**The Investigation:** Students explore structural properties of geometric shapes, then use index cards to make the tallest possible free-standing tower they can.

**NCTM Connections:** geometry • spatial reasoning • measurement

**Materials:** index cards• scissors • measuring tools
• Investigator's Log (p. 80) • Investigator's Wrap-Up (p. 81)

**Guide The Way**

⇨ Display some pictures of famous towers or skyscrapers so students can identify characteristic features they share. Guide them to notice geometric figures apparent in the structures, such as triangles or parallel lines.

⇨ Make sure students understand the parameters of this challenge: NOTHING but index cards and scissors. Provide MANY index cards so students can experiment with construction techniques before they attempt to build the actual structure. Encourage them to identify key shapes and arrangements that will result in taller, stronger structures.

⇨ Provide trays or large hard-bound books students can use as flat and portable "slab foundations" on which their structures can rest.

**Make The Connections**

⇨ Have students display their structures, explain their construction methods, and give the height. Peers can verify the measures.

⇨ Compile the height data on a class chart. Ask students to analyze the data to find average height (median, mean, or mode) and height range.

⇨ Invite students to contribute their structures to a class city—say, Indexiana. Students can examine the array of structures to find similarities, differences, patterns, or trends among them, as well as commonly used geometric shapes and construction techniques.

⇨ Extend by having students use only index cards to create the strongest possible "bridge" that spans at least 2 inches between books. They can arrange the cards any way they like EXCEPT stacking them. Determine the strongest bridge by how much weight it supports. Use small objects as units of measure, such as pennies, centimeter cubes, counters, or paper clips.

# Tower Power

## The Investigation:
How tall a structure can you build that can stand by itself?

The Eiffel Tower, the Sears Tower, the World Trade Center twin towers—you've seen these giants in photos. Maybe you've visited them. Creating tall buildings has challenged architects for decades. But you don't need concrete and steel to build the tallest structure in your classroom. All you need are index cards, a pair of scissors, an imagination, and some ideas on basic engineering and geometry.

### What To Do

**1** Get some index cards and a pair of scissors to build the tallest structure that stands by itself. Index cards are the ONLY construction material you may use—NO tape or glue, NOTHING but index cards. The structure must stand alone—that means NO holding it, NO leaning on something, NO supports of any kind.

**HINT:** Build on a tray or large book so you can easily move your structure.

**2** Figure out ways to connect cards. You may cut, fold, roll, stack, or attach them any way you can WITHOUT using other materials. Figure out what makes the cards sturdy and what doesn't work at all. Experiment!

**3** To count, your structure must stand by itself for at least one minute.

**4** Record the height of your structure to the nearest centimeter or quarter-inch. Notice the various geometric shapes that appear in the structure.

### Share Your Findings

**1** Present your structure to the class. Give its height. Tell what you discovered about arranging index cards to achieve the maximum height and strength.

**2** Add your structure to a class city, such as Indexiana. Examine the structures for similarities and differences. What construction ideas seem to work best?

# On a Roll

**The Investigation:** Students do an experiment to find out which weight and size of ball travels downhill the fastest.

**NCTM Connections:** statistics • geometry • computation • measurement • patterns and functions • proportional reasoning

***Materials:*** stopwatch • collection of balls • calculators • Investigator's Log (p. 80) • Investigator's Wrap-Up (p. 81)

**Guide The Way**

⇨ Begin by having students make predictions about which ball or balls will be the fastest and slowest. Have them record their predictions.

⇨ Emphasize the importance of testing each ball in the same way to make results as valid as possible.

⇨ Point out that trials may work best with three participants: one to roll the ball, one to catch it, and one to time it.

⇨ Review finding the range and averages of data, as needed. Have students debate whether the mean, median, or mode is the most useful gauge of the typical speed of each ball.

**Make The Connections**

⇨ Have students describe all aspects of their experiment and present their findings.

⇨ Encourage discussion of the findings by posing questions like these: *Which is the fastest ball? The slowest? What is the range of times for all balls? Which ball had the greatest range of times? What features of the balls affect their speed? How? What effects do degree of incline or ramp surface have on ball speed? Are these effects the same for all balls? What, if anything, about the results surprised you?*

⇨ If there are significant conflicting results, you might have students agree on an incline to use and retest together.

⇨ Extend by having students calculate the speed of the balls they test in feet per second or minute, or miles per hour.

Name: _____ Date: _____

# On a Roll

## The Investigation:
What kind of ball rolls downhill the fastest?

Will a basketball roll down a ramp faster than a tennis ball? What about a baseball? Will a golf ball beat them all? Or do all balls travel downhill at the same speed?

You can do an experiment to find out which size and weight of ball is the fastest.

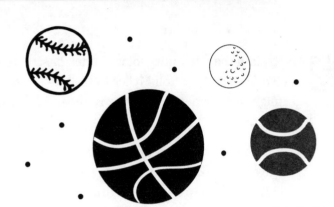

**What To Do**

**1** Gather a friend or two, a stopwatch or a watch with a second hand, and a collection of balls of different shapes and sizes.

**2** Make a ramp or choose an incline, such as a sloped driveway, a playground slide, or a seesaw. Set up a start line and a finish line. Measure the total length. Approximate the slope in degrees. Sketch the incline and label its dimensions.

**HINT:** To improve the accuracy of your measurements, practice rolling and timing the balls before you actually begin your experiment.

**3** Roll each ball down the incline five times. Record the time for each roll for each kind of ball.

**4** Find the range of times for each ball and for all the balls. Compute the average time for each ball and for all balls.

**5** Make a table to show your data. Be prepared to discuss any patterns you see.

**Share Your Findings**

**1** Display your results, which should include the labeled sketch of the incline you used and an organized list of the balls tested.

**2** Tell how you conducted your experiment. Describe all the factors involved. Present any conclusions you can draw from your data.

47

# Best Foot Forward

**The Investigation:** Students explore and analyze data about feet.

**NCTM Connections:** computation • estimation • measurement • statistics

***Materials:*** class name-lists • measuring tools • grid paper (pp. 82-83) • Investigator's Log (p. 80) • Investigator's Wrap-Up (p. 81)

**Guide The Way**

⇨ Explain that the unit *foot* was once based on the length of a king's foot. Read *How Big Is a Foot?* by Rolf Myller to the class. Ask students to imagine what problems might arise when people use nonstandard units of measure.

⇨ Distribute class name-lists for students to use as tables when recording their data.

⇨ Before this investigation, ask students to choose footwear they can easily remove. Have them examine their own feet and look at classmates' feet to make preliminary estimates. Then have them find the lengths of everyone's feet and display the data graphically. A histogram is an effective type of graph to use in this situation.

⇨ Brainstorm other ways to analyze class foot sizes. Ideas include finding various average lengths, average circumference of the ankle, or average width of the foot across its widest (or narrowest) part. Encourage students to suggest ideas. Have the class agree on several measures to investigate.

⇨ One way to find the area of the foot is to trace it on grid paper, then count full squares and combine partial ones. The following method may give a closer estimate: Draw the greatest polygonal figure that lies completely within the foot. Count its squares. Next, draw the smallest polygonal figure that completely encloses the foot. Then add half the number of squares in the region between the two polygons to the number of squares in the first polygon. Have students try both methods and compare results.

**Make The Connections**

⇨ Have students present the data and tell how they made their calculations. Have them compare their original estimates with the data they gathered.

⇨ Challenge students to draw the typical foot in the class, using their data.

⇨ Extend by having students investigate the average size of hands, heads, or length of arms, using many of the same techniques.

# Best Foot Forward

## The Investigation:
How long is a foot in your class?

You already know that a foot equals 12 inches. But is your own foot really a foot long? Is anyone's foot in your class a foot long? What variations are there among the feet you meet? Do a foot analysis to find out.

### What To Do

**1** Get an inch ruler to see exactly how long the unit 1 foot is. Estimate whether your foot (the one at the end of your leg!) is longer or shorter than 1 foot. Then measure to verify.

**2** Estimate how many of your classmates have feet exactly 1 foot long, less than 1 foot, and greater than 1 foot. Record your estimates to compare with the actual data you will collect later.

**HINT:**
To estimate the area of your foot, trace it on grid paper. Count full squares and combine partial squares.

**3** Find the actual lengths of feet in your class. Measure to the nearest quarter-inch. Make a table or graph to show the data.

**4** Find other ways to analyze foot size in your class. Here are some ideas: *What's the average area of a foot? What's the length of the typical big toe or pinky toe? What's the average width of a foot?*

**5** Compile all the data, complete your tables or graphs, and be ready to present your foot findings.

### Share Your Findings

**1** Present the data you found on feet. Compare the actual data with the estimates you made before you began to investigate. How accurate were your predictions?

**2** Tell how you found the area of a foot, which is an odd and curved shape.

# Left or Right?

**The Investigation:** Students predict and find percents of classmates who are right- and left-handed, right- and left-footed, and favor the right or left arm and thumb; they explore relationships among the data.

**NCTM Connections:** estimations • statistics • patterns and relationships • percents

**Materials:** class name-lists • calculators • circle graph (p. 84) • Investigator's Log (p. 80) • Investigator's Wrap-Up (p. 81)

## Guide The Way

⇨ Distribute class name-lists for students to use as tables when recording their data.

⇨ Discuss the idea that most people favor one hand over the other. Most people also favor one foot over the other when they kick or step. The dominant side is related to brain physiology, but people can learn to use one hand or foot more dominantly. The natural preferences people exhibit for folding arms and crossing fingers are genetically determined.

⇨ Be sure students understand the simple tests for determining the preferred side for hands, feet, arms, and thumbs. Help students plan an efficient method for gathering class data.

⇨ Help students create circle graphs to display the data. They can make four circle graphs, one each for hands, feet, arms, and thumbs; or two circle graphs, one for leftness and one for rightness.

⇨ Review the relationship among fractions, decimals, and percents, as needed. You may wish to review the use of the calculator for these computations.

## Make The Connections

⇨ Have students present their findings and explain how they figured them out. You might have peer partners verify each other's calculations.

⇨ Help students analyze the data to look for relationships by asking questions such as: *Are right-handed people usually right-footed? Is there a correlation between which thumb is on top and which arm is on top?*

⇨ Extend by having students investigate left-or-right preferences among students in other classes, among adults in the school community, or in other groups of people. They can make double bar graphs, circle graphs, or other kinds of visual aids to present comparative findings.

# Left or Right?

## The Investigation:
What percent of your classmates are left-footed?

Some people are right-handed, others are lefties. But did you know that people can be left- or right-footed? People can also be left- or right-thumbed, or favor their left or right arm. In this investigation, you'll find out which you and your classmates are.

**What To Do**

**1** Predict the percent of your class that is right-handed and left-handed. Then poll classmates to find the actual data. Use a table to record your data.

**2** Find your foot, arm, and thumb preferences. Your preferred foot is the one you kick with. Your preferred arm is the one that's on top when you fold your arms across your chest. Your preferred thumb is the one that's on top when you clasp your fingers. Try it and see! Record your findings in your table.

**3** Predict the percent of your class that's left-handed, right-handed, left-footed, right-footed, left-armed, right-armed, left-thumbed and right-thumbed. Then gather the actual data. Calculate each percent. Add this data to your table.

**4** Examine the data for relationships among hand, foot, arm, and thumb preferences. Find a way to graph the data. (HINT: Try circle graphs.) Prepare some statements you can share.

**HINT:** Keep track of each person's left-or-right preferences so you can look for relationships.

**Share Your Findings**

**1** Present your graphs and calculations. Explain how you reached your conclusions. Tell how you accounted for anyone who uses both hands (or feet) equally well.

**2** Discuss any relationships you noticed. For example: *Are right-handed people usually right-footed? Are any lefties right-thumbed?*

# The Ideal Athlete

**The Investigation:** Students explore physical characteristics of professional athletes to determine physical standards.

**NCTM Connections:** computation • statistics • measurement

*Materials:* calculators • collector cards, newspapers, sports magazines, and team programs • Investigator's Log (p. 80) • Investigator's Wrap-Up (p. 81)

**Guide The Way**

⇨ Point out that great skills, strong drive, and deep desire may not ensure professional success in sports. Tell students, for example, that the most coordinated, agile, and dedicated pitcher is unlikely to play professional baseball unless he or she can throw the ball at nearly 90 miles an hour.

⇨ Inform students that they needn't choose a *team* player to investigate, although it may be easier to find data about athletes on professional teams. Interested students may wish to research the physical characteristics of tennis players, gymnasts, skaters, runners, or other individual performers.

⇨ Help students brainstorm ways to locate the data they need.

⇨ You might group students by sport so they can share resources and discuss issues as they work.

⇨ Guide students to debate whether it makes more sense to identify the typical athlete by the *mean* of the data gathered or by the *mode*—the height, weight, etc., that occurs most often.

**Make The Connections**

⇨ Have students present their findings and explain how they figured them out. You might have students investigating the same sport verify each other's conclusions.

⇨ Extend by having students investigate a typical athlete in a different sport. Or they might try to characterize the ideal piece of sports gear, such as a hiking boot, baseball glove, or skateboard.

# The Ideal Athlete

**1 6 0 8 2 3**

## The Investigation:
How might you describe the ideal player in a sport?

For student athletes who dream of professional glory, talent isn't enough. Scouts for professional basketball teams won't even look at centers if they're much less than 7 feet tall. Football linemen must weigh at least 200 pounds to attract scouts. Pro teams generally look for talented young players who *also* match the physical profile of pro athletes at their position.

How can you identify the physical characteristics that describe the typical player at a particular position? You can gather data to find out.

**What To Do**

**1** Choose a sport you like. Identify a position that interests you. Select several professional players who play that position.

**2** Gather key physical data for each player—for example, height and weight. Use data from collector cards, sports magazines and newspapers, team programs and promotional materials, team Web sites, or other sources. Find data on the player's speed, strength, or any other attribute that's available for *all* players you're investigating.

**HINT:**
Find out what sports data classmates may already have and will share.

**3** Record your findings in a table.

**4** Use the data you've gathered to describe the *typical physical attributes* of professional athletes at that position. Write a summary of your findings.

**Share Your Findings**

**1** Distribute copies of your table for classmates to examine. Describe how you got your data. Share your conclusions. Invite responses and discussion.

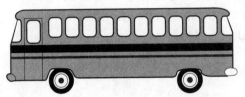

# How Much?
# How Many?
# How Far?

MOO!

# Dairy Diary

MOO!

**The Investigation:** Students analyze and compare dairy products.

**NCTM Connections:** statistics • measurement

***Materials:*** clean containers from dairy products • grid paper (pp. 82-83) • circle graph (p. 84) • protractor • Investigator's Log (p. 80) • Investigator's Wrap-Up (p. 81)

**Guide The Way**

➪ As students brainstorm kinds of dairy products, guide them to name generic products, such as yogurt or sour cream, rather than particular brands.

➪ You might suggest that some students compare variations of the same product, such as whole milk ricotta, part-skim ricotta, and fat-free ricotta, or compare similar products, such as hoop, farmer, and cottage cheeses.

➪ Help students read and understand the nutrition information provided on dairy product labels. Point out the importance of comparing same-size servings, because nutrition labels may present data based on servings of different sizes.

➪ If necessary, review the relationships among customary units of measure: ounce, cup, pint, quart, and gallon.

➪ Encourage students to present their data in circle graphs or in triple bar graphs to make comparisons readily apparent.

**Make The Connections**

➪ Have students present their graphs and findings and explain their procedures. Encourage students to pose questions and raise issues based on the dairy data to help them interpret the results.

➪ Invite students to make suggestions to the school cafeteria based on their findings, or prepare an informational newsletter for families that shares their findings.

➪ Extend by having students conduct a similar investigation of other categories of food, such as kinds of prepared foods, snack foods, or fast-food meals.

# Dairy Diary

## The Investigation:
In what ways can you compare dairy products?

Americans consume a variety of dairy products in a typical week—milk, cheese, yogurt, and butter, to name a few. We eat and drink these products because they're nutritional and they taste good (except for buttermilk...). But are all dairy products equally good for us? Keep a dairy diary to find out.

MOO!

**What To Do**

**1** Brainstorm to list as many different dairy products as you can. Visit the dairy department of a supermarket to jog your memory.

**2** Select three dairy products and plan to compare them. You might compare nutritional data, such as grams of protein, fat content, and so on. Or look at cost, shelf life, serving size, or any other factors you can think of to compare the products.

**HINT:**
Think about how you you could use triple-bar graphs or circle graphs to display dairy data.

**3** Gather your data. Get information from the containers of dairy products you have at home. Or visit a supermarket to collect data on the spot. Or consult a reference book for dairy data to support your investigation.

**4** Prepare a graph to present your findings. Include written information that summarizes what you discover. Be ready to field questions from classmates.

**Share Your Findings**

**1** Display your graph and explain how you came to your conclusions. Compare your findings with those of other students who investigated the same kinds of dairy products.

**2** Based on your data, propose recommendations you might make to consumers about their dairy decisions.

# Under Cover

**The Investigation:** Students estimate then calculate the percent of floor and wall space that's covered up in their classroom.

**NCTM Connections:** computation • estimation •measurement • percents • proportional reasoning • statistics

***Materials:*** calculators • measuring tools • circle graph (p. 84) • protractor • Investigator's Log (p. 80) • Investigator's Wrap-Up (p. 81)

**Guide The Way**

⇨ Discuss ways to estimate and calculate the area of an irregular region—in this case, a wall with doors or windows.

⇨ Point out that to estimate covered-up floor space, students need to imagine a bird's eye view of the floor.

⇨ Help students develop strategies for estimating percents visually. One method is to have students visualize how one half (50%) or one fourth (25%) looks. Then, they can use that amount of space as a benchmark against which to estimate the portion in question.

⇨ Suggest that students use multiplication and proportional reasoning when they calculate areas of repeated congruent shapes.

⇨ As needed, review the area formulas for various polygons and other figures. You might also review expressing fractions as percents and constructing circle graphs.

**Make The Connections**

⇨ Have students present their findings and graphs and explain how they obtained their data. You might have peer partners verify each other's calculations.

⇨ Invite students to express their findings as ratios—for example, the ratio of covered wall space to open wall space.

⇨ Extend by having students conduct a similar investigation of their room at home. Have them compare their findings to determine whether the percent of under-cover space is greater at home or in the classroom.

Name: _____     Date: _____

# Under Cover

## The Investigation:
What part of a room is under cover?

Look around at your classroom walls. What do you see? What do you *not* see?

Now notice the floor. Much of it appears to be out in the open. But if you could look down from above, you'd see that a lot of floor actually lurks under cover.

Find out how much of the room—the floor and the walls—is covered up.

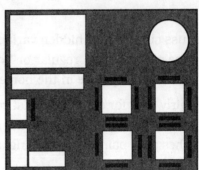

reading area

book shelf

computer & chair

book shelves

conferencing table

lab tables & chairs

**What To Do**

**1** Estimate the area of your classroom floor and walls. Then estimate the percent of each surface that is covered by pictures, bulletin boards, desks, tables, and so on. Don't count the space taken up by windows and doors because these don't actually cover any wall space. Record your estimates.

**2** Now calculate the actual total area of all floor space and wall space in the room. Also calculate the area of each surface that's covered. Then figure out the percent of the whole classroom that's under cover. Record your findings.

**3** Compare your findings with your estimates.

**HINT:**
Think of shortcuts to use to determine the total amount of space covered by same-size furniture or pictures.

**4** Make a circle graph to show your findings. Consider using sectors such as *Exposed Wall, Covered Wall, Exposed Floor, Covered Floor.*

**Share Your Findings**

**1** Present your estimate of what percent of wall and floor space is covered. Tell how you determined that figure. Then display your graph. Present your exact calculation of percent of covered space and tell how you found it.

**59**

# Go with the Flow

**The Investigation:** Students estimate the amount of water use in their home for one month.

**NCTM Connections:** estimation •measurement • computation • statistics

**Materials:** calculators • Investigator's Log (p. 80) • Investigator's Wrap-Up (p. 81)

**Guide The Way**

⇨ Discuss obvious and hidden variables that affect water use in any household, such as type of faucet (i.e., regular or "low-flow"), local water pressure, pipe diameter and age, number of people in the home, typical family habits and patterns, and so on.

⇨ It's fairly easy for students to list routine water-use activities, such as doing laundry or bathing. Guide them to consider less-frequent uses of water, such as washing brushes after painting or making a big pot of soup.

⇨ Help students determine sensible ways to estimate water use. For example, if they know that water flows at a rate of, say, 4 gallons per minute, and they usually take a 10-minute shower, then they can estimate that one shower uses about 40 gallons of water.

⇨ Review relationships among units of liquid measure: ounce, cup, pint, quart, and gallon.

**Make The Connections**

⇨ Have students present their findings and explain how they figured them out. You might have peer partners verify each other's estimates.

⇨ Some homes have water meters that register actual water use. To verify their estimates, students might ask an adult to show them a recent water bill. Or, they might learn to read their water meter to determine actual water use.

⇨ Invite an engineer or environmental scientist to address the class about the importance of water conservation. Encourage him or her to suggest ways to use less water.

⇨ Extend by having students conduct a similar investigation of electricity use.

# Go with the Flow

## The Investigation:
How much water does your family use in a month?

In most communities, people pay to get safe, clean water piped to their homes or businesses. Are you getting soaked by high water bills? Are you washing money down the drain? Tap your investigator's resources to figure out about how much $H_2O$ your family uses in a typical month.

**What To Do**

**1** Brainstorm ways your family uses water. Think about water use in different rooms, at different times of day, and by different family members. Consider regular and occasional use, indoor and outdoor use, and so on.

**2** When a tap is open, water flows out at about 3–5 gallons per minute. Use this fact to estimate water use for the activities on your list. Estimate in gallons or parts of gallons.

**HINT:** Remember, 4 cups = 1 quart, and 4 quarts = 1 gallon.

**3** Estimate total water use for a day. Then estimate water use for a month. Adjust the estimate to account for occasional water use, such as washing the dog or filling a new fish tank.

**4** Keep track of estimates and calculations you make along the way. Use them to support your thinking when you present your final estimate.

**Share Your Findings**

**1** Present your water use estimates to the class. Explain how you arrived at the figure.

**2** Compare your estimates with those of your classmates. Discuss why there are variations. Make a chart of water estimates. Analyze the data for high and low water use, range, and averages.

**3** Look back at the results. Where could you use less water? Brainstorm water-saving ideas.

# What's Inside?

**The Investigation:** Students explore the contents of packages of foods that come in different colors and shapes.

**NCTM Connections:** computation • estimation •measurement • statistics • probability • logic • percents

***Materials:*** grid paper (pp. 82-83) • circle graph (p. 84) • letter shell (p. 87) • calculators • protractor • Investigator's Log (p. 80) • Investigator's Wrap-Up (p. 81)

**Guide The Way**

⇨ Discuss the connection between gathering and examining empirical data, and making predictions based on that data.

⇨ This investigation works well for small groups of students who can share in the purchase, examination, analysis, and eating of the data!

⇨ Help students set up their bar graphs, as needed.

⇨ Review how to construct a circle graph. Suggest to students who investigate M & M's® or other multicolored products that they color the sectors of their circle graph to match the colors of the foods.

**Make The Connection**

⇨ Have students present their findings and explain how they conducted their investigation. If different groups investigated the same kind of product, you can compile class data from the data each has gathered.

⇨ Have students respond to questions like these: *Does each box have the same contents? If not, how do you explain this? What can you expect to find in a typical package of the product? How do you know? What would you expect the results to be if the entire school did this investigation? Why?*

⇨ Invite students to write to the manufacturer of the product they investigated to ask how each package is filled at the factory.

⇨ Extend by having students use their data to investigate probability. For example, using a bag of M & M's, they can find the probability of picking a red, of picking two blues in a row, of *not* picking a yellow, and so on.

# What's Inside?

**The Investigation:**
What's *really* inside a package of assorted goodies?

Some foods are more colorful than others, or come in different shapes. Some have more to say.

How many of each color are in a pack of M & M's®? In a bag of jelly beans? In a box of your favorite multi-colored cereal? How many different sayings are there in a bag of heart candies? Does each one appear the same number of times?

There's one way to find out—but it's better to investigate *after* lunch!

**What To Do**

**1** Choose one kind of candy, cereal, cookie, or snack that comes as an assortment. The assortment can be by color, shape, size, or any other distinguishing feature. Obtain <u>three</u> packages of it.

**2** Guess how many pieces are in the package. Then predict how many there are of each color or other feature. Record your guesses.

**HINT:**
To simplify making a circle graph, round percents to the nearest whole number.

**3** Spill out each package and sort its contents by distinguishing feature. Record your results in a chart.

**4** Make a triple bar graph to display your findings. Make one bar per package. Use as many sets of bars as there are features.

**5** Now find the percent of each feature for each package. Then find the mean percent for each feature. Use this data to construct a circle graph to display the contents of a typical package.

**6** Prepare a summary of your findings. Compare results with your predictions.

**Share Your Findings**

**1** Display your graphs and explain what each shows. Discuss any surprises or trends in the data.

**2** Predict the specific contents of a fourth package of the product you examined. Based on your data, what do you think will be inside? Explain.

**63**

# Counting the Uncountable

**The Investigation:** Students explore strategies for counting quantities that seem impossible to count, and then apply those strategies.

**NCTM Connections:** estimation • proportional reasoning • visual/spatial reasoning • computation

***Materials:*** bags of rice, lentils, unpopped popcorn, gravel, or other small objects • calculators • grid paper (pp. 82-83) • scale and measuring cups • Investigator's Log (p. 80) • Investigator's Wrap-Up (p. 81)

**Guide The Way**

⇨ For this investigation, provide rice, lentils, unpopped popcorn, aquarium pebbles, or other small objects that students can count.

⇨ Discuss the problems involved in trying to count large quantities. Invite students to give examples of large quantities of items they've tried to count, and any strategies they used to manage the task.

⇨ Encourage students to think of alternate ways to count the uncountable. Besides the grid method, students might count the number of rice grains that weigh, say, 1 gram, find the total number of grams in the box, then multiply. Others might suggest filling a small object, such as a thimble, with rice, count the grains, count the number of thimblefuls in the box, then multiply.

**Make The Connections**

⇨ Have students present their findings and explain their solution methods. Students who counted similar quantities of the same kind of object should compare and contrast their methods and results.

⇨ Extend by having students investigate how the police estimate the number of people in big crowds, such as at parades, political rallies, or outdoor concerts. They can also do research to find out how astronomers estimate the number of stars in the sky, how biologists estimate the number of bees in a hive or fish in a school, or other similar real-world counting situations.

Name: _____ Date: _____

# Counting the Uncountable

## The Investigation:
How can you count an amount that seems too hard to count?

How many blades of grass are on a lawn? How many people are in a *Where's Waldo?* scene? Impossible to know? Wrong! With some clever planning and good reasoning, it's possible to estimate such quantities. You can count on it!

**What To Do**

**1** Brainstorm some quantities that seem impossible to count, such as the number of grains in a box of rice or wildflowers in a field.

**2** Now think of ways to break each quantity into smaller parts. For example, picture laying a huge sheet of grid paper over a crowd and counting people in one small square. Where could this thinking lead?

**HINT:** Think about measuring tools that might help you, such as a scale or measuring cups.

**3** Develop a strategy for counting the uncountable. Try it with grains of rice, kernels of popcorn, lentils, or other small objects. Figure out a sensible way to estimate the total number of objects without actually counting them.

**4** Make a sketch that explains your method. Prepare a report on how you found the total. Be ready to demonstrate your plan and justify your reasoning.

**Share Your Findings**

**1** Present your sketch and demonstrate your method. Tell why your count seems reasonable.

**2** Talk about real-life situations in which this kind of counting is used.

# Bus Stop

**The Investigation:** Students explore ways to improve bus service in the community.

**NCTM Connections:** computation • estimation •measurement • percents

***Materials:*** local bus maps and schedules • calculators • grid paper (pp. 82-83) • Investigator's Log (p. 80) • Investigator's Wrap-Up (p. 81)

**Guide The Way**

⇨ Discuss the factors city planners must consider when designing bus routes. Talk about what's good and not so good about local service. If possible, invite a planner, bus driver, or dispatcher to visit the class and discuss route and service issues.

⇨ Provide local bus maps and schedules, and street maps of the community.

⇨ Help students figure out what to look for and where to go to make first-hand observations of service on a bus route.

⇨ Discuss ways to use percents to compare changes in numbers of buses, travel times, and numbers of stops. Talk about ways to use ratios to describe these differences.

⇨ If your community has other forms of public transportation, such as ferries or subways, you can have students focus on these instead. If your area has little or no public transportation, adjust the investigation to focus on road planning, or encourage students to create an entirely new bus system.

**Make The Connections**

⇨ Have students present and explain the bus information in their posters.

⇨ Invite students to propose their ideas to the local agencies in charge of bus service in your area.

⇨ Extend by having groups of students investigate designing a new network of bus routes for the whole town, city, or county. Investigate the use of computer software, such as *Sim City 2000*, to help students in their planning.

# Bus Stop

## The Investigation:

How can you design a better bus route?

Think about the buses that run in your area. Do they take you where you want to go? Do they come often enough? Do they keep to a schedule? Are there enough bus stops in reasonable places?

Maybe you can design a local bus route that works even better—for the community or...just for *you*.

### What To Do

**1** Choose one local bus. Trace its route on a bus or community map. Identify the starting and ending points and all stops. Figure out the length of the route.

**2** Investigate more about the route. Brainstorm ways to describe the service. Consider when buses run, how many are on the road, how long it takes to make a full circuit, and how much time passes between buses at a stop. Find answers by studying a bus schedule, asking a bus driver, or gathering data yourself.

**3** Once you've studied how things are, plan to make them better. If you want, be self-centered! Customize bus service to meet your needs and interests.

**4** Develop your plan to improve bus service. Then make a poster that presents an improved bus map and an improved schedule. Prepare a summary of the great changes you've made.

**HINT:**
If there is no public transportation in your area, take this opportunity to develop a plan for it!

### Share Your Findings

**1** Display your poster. Highlight the changes you've made in bus service.

**2** Analyze your new route and schedule mathematically. For instance, you might point out how many minutes are saved using the new route, or what percent of stops are at locations you use. Tell how your adjustments have improved service. Support your claims with the figures you've assembled. Then invite comments on your ideas.

# On the Road

**The Investigation:** Students explore travel options to distant locations.

**NCTM Connections:** computation • estimation •measurement • number sense • patterns and relationships

*Materials:* calculators • road atlases • travel books and brochures • Investigator's Log (p. 80) • Investigator's Wrap-Up (p. 81)

**Guide The Way**

⇨ Brainstorm exciting U.S. travel destinations. Suggest that students browse through the travel section of a newspaper or bookstore for inspiration.

⇨ Discuss the ups and downs of different transportation options. Encourage students to consider factors other than cost and speed when making their choices. For instance, they might think about the pleasures of taking scenic routes or of being able to stop at interesting places along the way.

⇨ Be sure students understand that their task is to plan *only* the travel part of their trip. However, if they consider a long car trip, meals on the road and overnight accommodations will necessarily become part of the plan.

⇨ Provide guidebooks or travel brochures to help students find locations and costs of motels and restaurants along their route.

⇨ Guide students to use common sense as well as number sense in their plans. For example, point out that it would be impractical to drive for twenty-four hours straight, or to arrive at a national park at 2:00 AM!

⇨ Review map reading skills, as needed.

**Make The Connections**

⇨ Have students display and explain their charts and describe their travel plans. Ask volunteers to go over their proposed trip step-by-step, explaining each cost and how long each leg of the trip will take. Invite listeners to ask questions and make suggestions.

⇨ Have students talk about the factors that affect travel cost, such as low- or high-season travel, non-stop vs. direct flights, full fares vs. special discounts, and so on.

⇨ Extend by having students investigate the United States interstate highway system. Have them carefully examine a road atlas to figure out how roads are numbered. For instance, there are patterns in the numbers of east/west and north/south highways, for highways that bypass cities, and for those that go right through them.

# On the Road

## The Investigation:
How can you get to where you want to go?

From the rain forests on Washington's Olympic Peninsula to the Everglades in South Florida, there are hundreds of great places to visit in the United States. Where do *you* want to go?

Like a travel agent, make arrangements for a one-way trip— to the destination of your choice.

**What To Do**

**1** Pick an exciting place to go that's far from home. Assume you'll travel with one adult who can drive.

**2** Investigate travel options—plane, bus, train, car, boat, or combinations of them. Or be creative! Consider unusual travel options, such as bicycle, helicopter, or horseback.

**3** Contact airline, train, rental car, and bus companies for information. Study maps and travel pamphlets. Learn about costs, schedules, and travel times. Consider hidden costs and disadvantages of each travel option you explore. But don't forget to weigh the benefits, too.

**HINT:** Account for all hidden costs— getting to and from the airport, gas and tolls, food and motels along the way on a car trip, etc.

**4** Chart your findings. Include the total cost and time needed for each *complete door-to-door* trip for you and one adult. Break the trip into its parts—for example, taxi to airport, plane to destination city, rental car to final spot.

**5** Select the plan you like best. Prepare a travel summary that describes it in detail. Prepare a list of reasons for your choice.

**Share Your Findings**

**1** Describe your destination and tell why you chose it. Then show your chart and point out its key features. Explain how you obtained your data.

**2** Present your travel summary. Include all phases, costs, and times. Tell why you chose this plan. Explain why you rejected other options.

# Stating Data

**The Investigation:** Students use the Internet to gather, organize, and analyze data on the United States.

**NCTM Connections:** technology • statistics • logical reasoning • patterns and relationships

*Materials:* computers with modems • chart paper • atlases and state maps • letter shell (p. 87) • Investigator's Log (p. 80) • Investigator's Wrap-Up (p. 81)

**Guide The Way**

⇨ Discuss the kinds of data readily available about the fifty United States. Help students identify useful sources for this information, such as almanacs, encyclopedias, geography books, and atlases.

⇨ Explain that students can use the speed and diversity of the Internet to gather data from people around the country. If necessary, get help from computer-literate students, teachers, or parents in your school community to establish Internet access for posting and retrieving data online. Some useful Web sites include Classroom Connect (http://www.classroom.net), Global SchoolNet Foundation (http://gsn.org), and Scholastic Network (http://Scholastic.com/network). You can also e-mail to KIDSPHERE-request@vim.cis.pitt.edu.

⇨ To get responses that can be quantified and compared, all students must ask the same questions in the same ways. Have the class agree on questions everyone will explore. Guide students to word each question clearly and simply to elicit focused responses they can easily evaluate.

⇨ You might assign particular states or groups of states to different students or groups. Each group can then contribute its findings to the entire project.

⇨ You might help students use database or spreadsheet software to organize and present their findings. Some students may be able to present data in interesting graphical formats. Encourage them to be creative and to take advantage of the computer software with which they are familiar.

**Make The Connections**

⇨ Have students present their findings. You might set up a USA display visitors can enjoy over several days or weeks.

⇨ Discuss with students interesting ways to share their findings beyond the classroom. For instance, they might contact a local or state tourist agency, a relocation company, or public service organizations that might be interested in having kid-friendly information to share with their clients.

⇨ Extend by having students write questions for a USA game show, the answers to which appear somewhere in the display.

#  Stating Data

**The Investigation:**
How can you gather and display interesting statistical data about the United States?

Sure, you know there are fifty states. Maybe you can name them all, and their capitals. You could find the population of some of America's largest cities. But what other kinds of statistics can you gather about the USA? How can you organize, analyze, and display it for others to enjoy? In this investigation, you'll collect data you can use to describe America in ways that will appeal to other kids. You'll travel the nation without leaving home!

**What To Do**

**1** Brainstorm kinds of data you can easily gather on the USA. Flip through an almanac for ideas.

**2** Now think of more unusual facts you'd like to know. Be creative! For different states, you might wonder the price of a movie ticket, the day school starts, or the cost of printing a 24-shot roll of film. Develop a survey of 5-10 questions people can answer with numerical data on their states.

**3** For fun, add 2 or 3 offbeat questions, such as: *How many steps are there in front of your state's capitol building?* or *What community in your state has the longest name?*

**4** Write a letter that tells the purpose of the survey. Post the letter and the survey on the Internet. Ask people from different states to reply.

**5** As replies come back, sort and organize them. Design charts or graphs to display the data. When you have all your data, prepare a report to share with your class, your school, and Internet correspondents.

**HINT:** You can use a school or a home computer for this project. Ask adults who have computers for their help.

**Share Your Findings**

**1** Share the results of your survey with your classmates.

**2** Examine the data to look for trends, similarities, and differences.

**3** Publish your findings on-line, around your school, or in your community.

# Run and Jump

**The Investigation:** Students explore the correlation, if any, between running distance and jumping length in the long jump.

**NCTM Connections:** computation • estimation • measurement • statistics

**Materials:** measuring tools • long-jump runway and landing area • grid paper (pp. 82-83) • Investigator's Log (p. 80) • Investigator's Wrap-Up (p. 81)

**Guide The Way**

⇨ Provide students with data on long-jump records and the standard length of the long-jump runway. Invite a track coach to clarify this information with the class, as well as to discuss key safety issues and some style elements of the sport. The coach can describe how to measure the length of a jump. If possible, show a video of a long jump competition.

⇨ Assist students in setting up the investigation. One way is to have a team of students measure out pre-chosen distances along the runway and past it, as needed. Students unable to participate in the jumping can help with making measurements or graphing data.

⇨ Guide students to realize that this investigation isn't meant for competition among classmates, but rather to explore a possible correlation between length of a take-off run and length of the jump. Hopefully, students will determine the ideal length of a take-off run, one that provides adequate momentum but avoids overtiring the jumper.

⇨ Review how to make and interpret a *scatterplot*. This is a useful tool for displaying and analyzing all class data. Help students understand how a scatterplot can show positive and negative correlations among data.

**Make The Connections**

⇨ Have students present their findings and explain what they learned about a relationship between running distance and jumping length. Ask them to compare their results with their predictions.

⇨ Make a scatterplot together to display class results. Have students analyze it to determine the optimum distance for a long-jump runway for the class.

⇨ Extend by challenging students to discover the distance over which they run their fastest. They start by marking off distances in 20-yard increments from 20 to 100 yards. Students run each distance (20, 40, 60, 80, and 100 yards) separately, one time each. They time each run, and use proportional reasoning to find their running speed (in miles per hour or feet per second). To eliminate the fatigue factor that could skew the data, students should not run all five races consecutively. When they do finish, have them share their results and draw conclusions from them.

# Run and Jump

## The Investigation:
### How far do you have to run in order to jump the farthest?

You've probably seen Olympic athletes sprint down a runway before leaping amazing lengths. And you may know from experience that you can jump farther with a running start than you can from standing still. So, can you conclude that the farther you run before jumping, the farther you'll jump? Do an experiment to find out.

**What To Do**

**1** Work with a partner. Use a long-jump runway and landing area at a local athletic field. Or, set up a homemade landing area on any level field.

**2** Predict the running distance that will give you your best jump.

**3** Stand on the take-off board. Make your best leap. Measure the distance. Jump and measure again. Record the greater jump.

**HINT:** If a jump is "foul," just try again. There's no penalty!

**4** Try two more jumps, now using a running start from 10 feet back. Record the longer of these two leaps.

**5** Try other pairs of jumps, each pair starting from a different distance behind the take-off board. For example, jump after running 25 feet, 50 feet, 75 feet, and 100 feet. Then try starting from even farther back—125 feet or 150 feet. Record the distance of the better leap in each set of jumps you make.

**6** Graph your results. Describe what you discovered about the relationship between runway distance and jump length.

**Share Your Findings**

**1** Display your graph and describe the data it shows. Tell what you learned about the ideal length for a long-jump runway designed for you.

**2** Tell about the problems you encountered in setting up and carrying out this investigation. Explain how you addressed each one.

# Fold and Fly

**The Investigation:** Students explore constructing paper airplanes to optimize the distance flown; they plan and conduct a contest and analyze the results.

**NCTM Connections:** spatial reasoning • geometry • statistics • measurement

*Materials:* paper • assorted connecting materials (tape, paper fasteners, paper clips, etc.) • measurement tools • grid paper (pp. 82-83) • Investigator's Log (p. 80) • Investigator's Wrap-Up (p. 81)

**Guide The Way**

⇨ This investigation will work best as a whole-class activity. Discuss safety rules for constructing and flying paper airplanes. Establish guidelines that will encourage cooperation with and consideration for others, as well as fairness and fun throughout the investigation.

⇨ Demonstrate some simple ways to make paper airplanes. A good resource is *The Paper Airplane Book* by Seymour Simon. Students might try making different planes at home to settle on a design they like best, and fine-tune it in preparation for the contest.

⇨ Work with students to set fair contest rules. For example, discuss whether to measure distance at the farthest point a plane reaches while still airborne, the spot where it touches down, or the point where it comes to rest. Alternately, students might measure flight *duration* rather than distance.

⇨ Hold the contest indoors to avoid wind gusts. The gym, cafeteria, or other large room or corridor may work best. Close windows, if possible. Help students design the "runway." Use tape to designate a take-off line and boundaries, if needed.

⇨ Review measuring to the nearest $1/4$ inch or nearest millimeter, if necessary. Discuss which measure of central tendency best describes the contest results.

**Make The Connections**

⇨ Have students discuss the graph of distances achieved in the contest. Have them find the range of flight distances and the average distance flown. Ask them to explain "outlying" data, if any.

⇨ Discuss ways to improve the rules of the contest, if it were held again.

⇨ Tell the class that in 1995, university students in the Netherlands built and flew a paper airplane whose wing span was nearly 46 feet. It traveled 114 feet indoors! Extend this investigation by having students try to build the largest possible paper airplane that can fly.

# Fold and Fly

## The Investigation:
How far can you make a paper airplane fly?

In 1933, a paper airplane reportedly flew more than a mile! It was launched from an office building in Manhattan and floated across the East River to Brooklyn. The longest paper airplane flight indoors—193 feet—was recorded in 1985. How close you may come to these amazing world records depends on your creativity, your folding and engineering skills, and your launch technique.

**What To Do**

**1** Design a paper aircraft that can fly. You may use any kind of paper, as well as tape, paper clips, or any other common materials that may help your plane go farther.

**2** Make your plane. Do some test flights. Try to improve the distance the plane can go by noticing how it flies and adjusting its design or your launch style.

**3** Plan a paper airplane contest. Set up an indoor "runway" in the gym or in a long corridor. Determine contest rules. Mark a take-off line, side boundaries, and establish a way to measure distance flown. Hold some practice flights to fine-tune the runway, the rules, and the measuring methods.

**4** Hold the contest. Record all distances flown.

**5** After the contest, graph the results. Examine the graph for patterns. Be prepared to discuss your findings.

**HINT:** Decide what part of the plane to measure to and how accurately to measure—to the nearest millimeter or 1/4 inch, for example.

**Share Your Findings**

**1** Display the graph. Find the range of flight distances and the average distance flown. Find out how close the best flight came to the world record. (Contact *The Guinness Book of Records*, if necessary!)

**2** If possible, explain why some planes flew farther than others. Invite successful plane makers to describe their techniques.

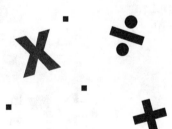

# Appendix

# ▣ xtra ▣ deas

**Here are some more ideas for real-life math investigations to explore with your students. Develop these ideas more completely, or simply provide the kernel of the idea and have students take it from there!**

➡ **1** Do a survey on a topic that interests you. Pose a series of questions and plan for the responses. Then conduct the survey and organize, display, and analyze the results.

➡ **2** Investigate stats on bats or other sports gear that comes in different sizes, lengths, shapes or weights.

➡ **3** Plan a class trip or excursion. Figure out the whole deal—total cost, schedule, means of transportation, meals or snacks, materials or supplies needed, cost per mile traveled, adult-to-student ratio, etc.

➡ **4** Investigate glyphs. Find out what they are and how to use them. Create glyphs to display data about the class. (See *Teaching Children Mathematics* [the journal of the National Council of Teachers of Mathematics], February 1996, page 324, for ideas.)

➡ **5** Design an original screen-saver for a computer. Use mathematical ideas, such as symmetry, tessellations, tangrams, transformations, recursions, or other applications of math in art.

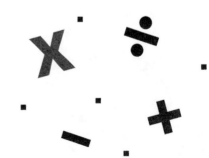

# Extra Ideas *(Cont.)*

**6** What kind of ball is easiest to shoot into a basket? Examine typical balls that have recognizable sizes and shapes, such as a football, soccer ball, tennis ball, golf ball, handball, and beach ball.

**7** Suppose you won a million dollar jackpot (lucky you!). Determine the best way to take your winnings—all at once, or in weekly, monthly, or yearly installments. Make a budget to show your solution.

**8** How much does it really cost to serve a balanced meal for four people? Plan a healthy meal menu for one breakfast, one lunch, and one dinner. Plan reasonable serving sizes. Then calculate the cost of everything.

**9** How many boxes would it take to move all the stuff in your room at home or at school? Determine how to pack everything, how many boxes it would take, how long it would take to pack, and how much to budget for boxes, tape, and other supplies.

**10** Which long-distance company in your area has the best rates? Decide on hypothetical calls to 5 different long-distance destinations. Then find the price for each call at the rates charged by each company. Compare the companies. Which one would you choose and why?

Name: _____ Date: _____

# Investigator's Log

**Investigation** _____
_____

**Questions to ask** _____
_____
_____
_____
_____

**Details to explore** _____
_____
_____
_____
_____

**Sources of information** _____
_____
_____
_____
_____

**Sketches**

Name: _____    Date: _____

# Investigator's Wrap-Up

**Investigation** _____

_____

**How I got my solution** _____

_____

_____

_____

**What I learned** _____

_____

_____

_____

**Problems I encountered** _____

_____

_____

_____

**Questions that came to mind** _____

_____

_____

_____

**How I used math ideas** _____

_____

_____

_____

**What I'd do differently next time** _____

_____

_____

Quarter-Inch Grid Paper

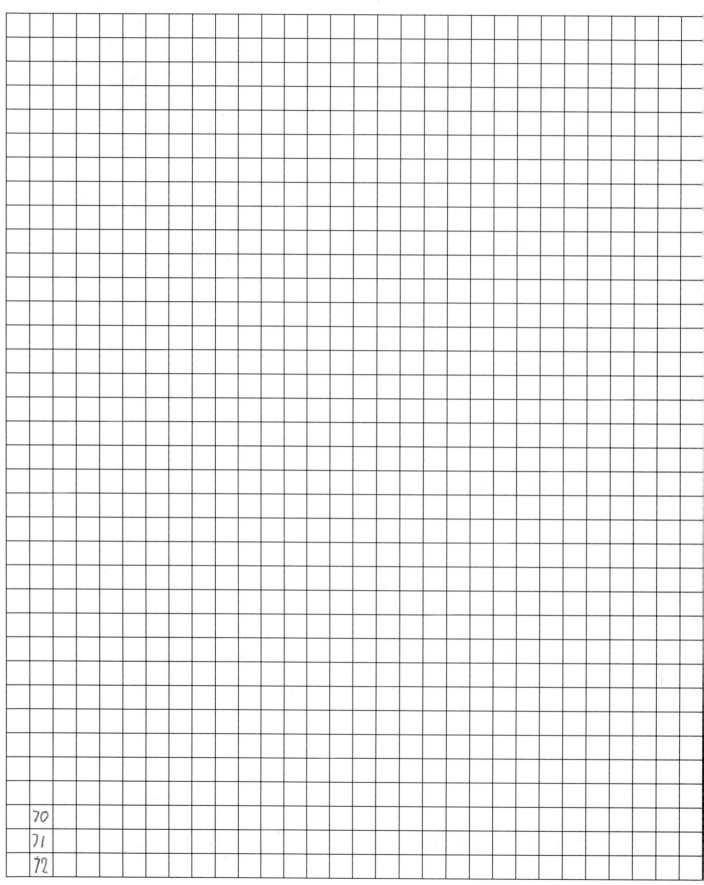

70
71
72

**82**

36
+36

Centimeter Grid Paper

**83**

# Circle Graph

# Tally Table

| | Tallies | Totals |
|---|---|---|
| | | |
| | | |
| | | |
| | | |
| | | |
| | | |
| | | |
| | | |
| | | |
| | | |
| | | |
| | | |
| | | |
| | | |
| | | |
| | | |
| | | |
| | | |
| | | |
| | | |
| | | |
| | | |

# Venn Diagram

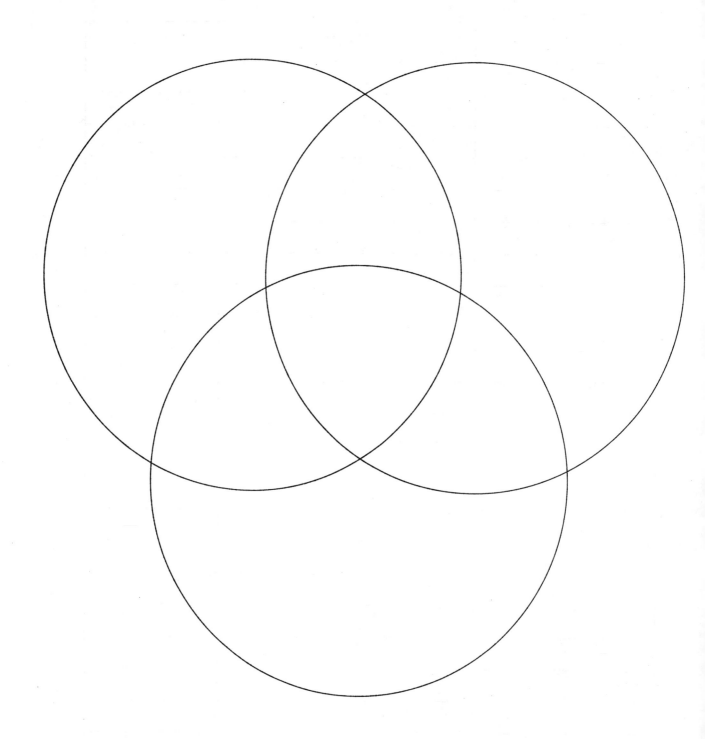

#  Letter Shell

_____

_____

_____

_____

_____

_____

_____

_____

**Dear** _____ :

_____

_____

_____

_____

_____

_____

_____

_____

_____

_____

_____

_____

_____

_____

**Yours truly,**

_____